# Coaching Champions

# Coaching Champions

*How to Get the Absolute Best
Out of Your Salespeople*

Frank Salisbury, Cariona Neary,
and Karl O'Connor

Oak Tree Press
19 Rutland Street,
Cork, Ireland.

http://www.oaktreepress.com

© 2001  Frank Salisbury, Cariona Neary and Karl O'Connor

A catalogue record of this book is
available from the British Library.

ISBN 1 86076 203 4

Printed in the Republic of Ireland by Techman Ltd.

# Contents

# About the Authors

**Frank Salisbury** is a director of Softsell, based in Oxford, and of Business and Training Solutions, based in Dun Laoghaire, County Dublin; and a partner of The Salisbury Partnership based in Banbury, along with his wife Pauline and their son Michael. These companies specialise in sales process and point of sale design, sales training, and sales coaching. He also operates as a personal coach for senior executives. In 1990, he completed his MPhil on the subject of "The Effectiveness of Sales Training". He has written two editions of *Sales Training*, the second of which was published by Gower in 1999. His first book on coaching was *Developing Managers as Coaches*, published by McGraw-Hill in 1994. Frank and Pauline live in Oxfordshire and in Dublin. Their daughter Helen has worked for the Partnership and now also lives in Dublin.

**Cariona Neary** is an international business consultant and trainer with expertise in the field of transnational marketing and personal development. She is an associate tutor with the Irish Management Institute as well as Director of Campaigns with the Irish Exporters Association. She also worked for over ten years with the German-Irish Chamber of Industry and Commerce where she provided consultancy and training on market entry strategies and cross-cultural communications. She holds a degree in Business Studies from the University of Limerick and the Graduateship in Marketing, awarded by the Marketing Institute of Ireland, as well as a number of diplomas for German and French. Cariona is the author of three distance learning programmes in marketing and in customer care and is editor of a direct marketing journal as well as contributing regularly to specialist marketing magazines. She co-founded Ireland's first direct marketing certificate, sponsored by the Irish Direct Marketing Association (IDMA) and has lectured in the fields of communication and international marketing. She has also acted as Examiner for a number of professional education bodies.

**Karl O'Connor** is Senior Manager (Training and Development) with First Active plc. He has worked in financial services for 19 years and has won national and international awards for excellence in human resource management. He is Chairman of the Institute of Bankers (Dublin Region). Karl has lectured in several Irish universities and management institutes and holds a business degree from the University of Limerick and a Masters degree from University College Dublin. He has published articles in several trade journals and contributed to *The Irish Employee Recruitment Handbook*, which was published by Oak Tree Press in 1999. Karl is a member of the Irish Institute of Training and Development and a Fellow of the Chartered Institute of Personnel and Development (CIPD). He is a regular presenter on several CIPD courses.

# Acknowledgements

I should like to take this opportunity to thank my colleagues at Business and Training Solutions in Dublin, Softsell in Oxford, and the sales managers of The Chelsea Building Society in Cheltenham for their invaluable help during the various stages of research for this book.

*Frank Salisbury*

I would like to acknowledge the help and inspiration I have received through working with Julie Ryan of the Irish Management Institute and my former colleagues at the German-Irish Chamber of Industry and Commerce.

*Cariona Neary*

To all the managers I have trained and coached, thank you. You have taught me about life and the need for continuous learning.

*Karl O'Connor*

# Dedications

For Pauline, Michael and Helen

To Ashling, Aoife and our parents Esther, Paddy and Breeta

# Chapter 1

# The Seeds of Greatness

*"No one's so good, they can't get better"* — Nick Faldo

## The Challenge

Nick Faldo's comment on the world of golf can be equally applied in the business world. It's a statement that must have a special resonance for sales managers as they face year after year of ever-tougher targets. How can you continue to improve? And how can you get your top performers to do even better, reach even higher targets? Sales managers face enormous challenges in harnessing their team and driving them towards a goal of continuous improvement. Indeed, one of the greatest issues today is to recruit and retain good salespeople. Top performers who do not feel challenged or acknowledged vote with their feet in markets where their skills and talents are in strong demand.

## You Can Make the Difference!

All the evidence points to one fact: the manager can make the difference between the performance of a good team and that of an outstanding team. Exit interviews conducted in many organisations before people leave their employers have highlighted that people don't leave jobs because they were unhappy with the company; they leave because they were unhappy with their manager. But this is a two-sided coin. If you have the skills to lead, motivate, challenge and share your vision with your team, then you are on the road to higher productivity, higher profitability and higher customer satisfaction, as well as higher staff retention. Easy? No: it takes a fundamental shift in the way you lead your team. It is about taking a journey, starting with yourself and your own barriers to greater performance.

For some people, it is a long and sometimes winding road that leads them to embrace the concept of coaching. This book provides a roadmap to the concept and application of coaching.

Coaching is based on the premise that we all have talents and abilities that are unrealised. Just as our sales team is made up of individuals whose full potential is as yet untapped, the same is true of sales managers. We must learn the core skills of coaching: questioning, listening, observing, and providing feedback. We need to examine our attitudes towards people's potential and we need to learn how to develop a new foundation for our relationship with our team. Such a relationship must be based on the learner taking responsibility for their own performance, on increased self-awareness of the learner and on trust and belief rather than blame and recrimination.

### From Sports Coach to Management Coach

Do you need to hold an Olympic Gold Medal in long-distance running to be able to coach Sonia O'Sullivan or Catherina McKiernan? Do you need to have a bagful of caps for Ireland to be able to coach the Munster rugby team? We accept that in the sports world, great coaches must be just that: great coaches. We don't expect them to have achieved all the goals they set for the sports people they are coaching. Yet in business, we believe the most effective sales trainers should have a track record as successful salespeople. Why?

Whilst many of us have had the misfortune of meeting mediocre trainers who lacked the requisite job knowledge and application, the experience of working on the coaching model in this book has thrown into some doubt the theory that you must first be a practitioner before you become a trainer. In the years since Frank Salisbury first developed his POWER© coaching model, he has coached people to play better snooker and golf — even though his own skills in both leave a lot to be desired! There are many examples of leaders from the worlds of the creative arts and sports improving the skills of business managers using coaching techniques, without themselves having been in management. Granted, coaches need knowledge of the job to be done, but they need to be neither proficient nor expert in the role being coached. However, the person being coached must have a basic knowledge or understanding of the skill before coaching can commence.

Coaching is a development tool that can only be productive after skills training has taken place. A salesperson who has just been appointed to the job cannot be coached to achieve stretching targets without some basic training being provided in the first instance — for example, in product knowledge. Those operating as trainers, in most cases, need to have first-hand experience of the job, while those coaching require different attributes and skills.

As in sports, coaching in business is about winning. The sales manager is responsible for winning, for keeping their people focused on goals, for nurturing their self-belief and for motivating them to become champions in their field.

**Coaching — A Definition**

In his book *Developing Managers as Coaches*, Frank Salisbury has defined coaching as:

> The release of latent talent and skills, previously un-tapped by training, through a process of self-awareness initiated by the coach.

We all have latent talent and skills. For a myriad of reasons, some people are able to tap into some of that latent talent and skill, but most do not. For the latter, that lack of usage over a period of time may make it appear as though it never existed in the first place.

Companies spend small and even large fortunes employing people only to see them either fail completely or simply fail to deliver on previously held high expectations. We do not view this failure as the fault of the individual, at least not until they realise their complicity, but of the training and management process following employment.

One of the biggest reasons for lack of success in a role during a probationary period is poor induction. Induction either happens in the field or at the workplace with a manager. It can happen that, within a day of starting, a new employee, under the guidance of a manager, is either shown how to fail, or how not to succeed. Think about it.

## Training versus Coaching

If you accept, and the evidence leaves one no choice, that the manager is a key influence on the performance of their team, then where does that leave training? Sales managers will often blame the training function for their team's underperformance. Yet we are convinced that training fails to deliver primarily due to line management's apathy and the lack of support for field training activities. However, line management is not solely responsible for this situation. The problem is exacerbated by the trainer's inability to show the manager any real lasting benefit from training. Trainers and managers are as far apart from each other these days as they have ever been, each blaming the other for performance shortfalls in trainees. From the two seemingly opposing camps, one commonly hears remarks such as the following:

- *Managers*: "If those people in training only came down from their ivory towers and tried dealing with reality it might do them a world of good."

- *Trainers*: "What's the point of training anybody simply to send them into the clutches of a management team oblivious to the needs of continuous training?"

Neither attitude is helpful, either to the relationship between trainers and managers or to the organisation and the rest of the people working in it.

What coaching has done for us — and it can do the same for you — is to bring managers and trainers together, focusing on a common goal, using the same ball, and playing as a team on a level playing field. By using a common philosophy and language, we have observed a change in the manager/trainer relationship that produces in each a trust of the skills that each player has and the desire of each to excel and to have their charges excel, the premise being that each person can excel at a job, given the opportunity and assistance to do so.

In terms of the skills we have and can acquire, at the moment of birth we are all equal. We have our parents' genes, but external factors being equal, we all have the same opportunity for greatness. Those external factors, such as family and schooling, soon play a major role in influencing our journey and eventual destination.

These and other similar self-evident truths aside, it is clear that managers, computer programmers, doctors, lawyers, clerks, drivers, salespeople, and a thousand other job-holders, whether classified as professionals or not, are not born to those professions, but are fabricated into them by their environment and chance. Correspondingly, road sweepers, ditch diggers, the unemployed and the unemployable are not products of genetic certainty, but of circumstance, opportunity and, most importantly, the loving care and attention given to their seeds of greatness, or perhaps the lack of it.

As George Eliot put it: "It is never too late to be what you might have been."

All employees have it within themselves to deliver personal performances of excellence beyond their currently perceived limits of aspiration. Our contention, supported by our own experience and practical research into management, is that people at work have greater aspirations than either the manager realises, or than those they are willing to share with their man-

ager. We propose that the manager who operates as a coach
can bring the seed of greatness to the surface in all its glory.
We are not inviting managers to lead from behind, but to rid
themselves of the normal managerial trait of *telling*. By adopting the principles espoused in this book, they can reap the harvest of the seeds of greatness within their staff.

## The Telling Trap

It may seem a simple piece of advice to put into action, but in
our experience one of the greatest challenges for managers
and trainers in adopting the principles of coaching is to give up
telling other people what to do — when appropriate. Managers
and trainers seem to find it difficult to know when it is not appropriate. Phrases like "She's a natural leader", "He takes
charge immediately", "They lead from the front" and so on advocate that leading and managing is about telling people what
to do. It's a natural enough phenomenon. We grow up being
told what to do by our parents; it is something we expect. It is
hardly surprising, therefore, that as parents we then fall into the
telling trap ourselves. Many may argue that this is necessary.
What is certainly neither necessary nor desirable is that when
we become *managers*, we tend to constantly tell others what to
do. Certainly there are occasions when telling is required. A
new employee needs to be told and shown what to do on the
job and how to do it. Coaching someone through an emergency
is not appropriate and although it may result in empowerment
of the individual, it might also lead to tears and injury.

The educational system, from primary to secondary school,
continues the process of telling begun by our parents and, for
the vast majority of people, entry into the labour market ex-
poses us to yet further instructions. Those leaving secondary
school and entering the more liberal environment of colleges
and universities experience self-directed learning for the first
time, where students must take responsibility for their own
education. However, the patterns of interaction in a learning
environment set down in those early years are a form of mental

programming which is difficult to change in later life. Newly appointed managers often do not receive appropriate formal training regarding their new role, so they slip back into the old habits of telling, which implies, "I know best, so let me do the thinking." Can we really expect outstanding performance from people who don't even get a chance to shape their own goals?

## Coaching is not Counselling

Many managers confuse coaching with being soft, showing weakness when what is required is strength. Coaching is not a soft option. It requires strength of character. It requires managers to be strong in their belief that employees have the solution to their performance problems within them. It requires that managers have the courage to let go.

Coaching is also confused with counselling. It can be similar, but it is not the same. The British Association for Counselling (BAC) defines counselling as:

> . . . the skilled and principled use of the relationship to facilitate self-knowledge, emotional acceptance and growth, and the optimal development of personal resources.

In coaching, as in counselling, the answer to performance problems and potential lies within each individual, and as with the counsellor, those answers can be extracted by careful and systematic questioning. To that end, coaching also seeks to bring about self-awareness in the performer (the term we will use for the person being coached). In coaching roles within organisations, however, the coach has a clear objective to focus people on performance issues. The coach has a goal, and that goal is almost always tied in with organisational objectives. Managers as coaches also have an additional responsibility and accountability and are therefore additionally concerned with timescales. The seed of greatness has to be tended and nurtured, but it also has to provide and deliver.

Coaches are not counsellors. The difference between coaching and counselling is that coaching focuses on individual and ultimately organisational performance while counselling is focused on the individual alone. As a business coach you have a responsibility to move people forward towards a corporate aim. That movement forward involves expense in, for example, management and salesperson time if results are not being achieved. The company coach, therefore, is acutely aware of when to pull the plug if results are not being achieved, following this mutual investment in time through the application of POWER© coaching. A counsellor does not have that responsibility. You may have the desire to move people forward, but the responsibility for the timescale rests with the individual.

### COUNSELLING VS COACHING

| Counselling Focus | Coaching Focus |
|---|---|
| Individual | Individual and organisation |
| Problems | Opportunities |
| Past | Future |
| Time set by individual | Agreed timescale |

Counselling is focused on helping the individual to overcome problems encountered, while coaching is geared towards developing the performer to realise future opportunities.

### Concept, Practice, Process

This book is about a new way of developing, managing and empowering people. It is about adopting coaching as a concept, a practice and a process. It is a way of thinking which should be embodied within your own beliefs about people and their untapped abilities.

The concept holds that most people want to contribute more than they currently are allowed to, that they want to belong and be in control of their own destinies, but that somewhere along the journey they were hijacked.

The practice requires transference from the theory of the classroom to the reality of work. It requires managers to release people from the chains of telling and of rules and regulations and conformity. It requires managers to understand that subordinates have the same feelings of responsibility as they do, and that trust is something to be shared — it is a two-way process. But trusting is a risky business which takes time to build — "I tried that once and it didn't work!" — so try it again until it does.

## Anyone Can Be a Coach!

This book is written specifically for people in sales and sales management. Whether as coach or as someone being coached, there should be something here for you. Anyone can be a coach, in any situation, providing there exists a genuine desire to adopt these coaching principles. There also needs to be a shared vision, trust, and mutual support. Furthermore, coaches need to believe in the premise that all people can grow. The coach has to have a clear vision of that growth, both for themselves and the people they work with. The greatest gift a coach can give is time — time to coach.

In this book, we will explore the need for managers as coaches to be aware of the levels of competence in their salespeople as they acquire new skills and insights, moving from a state of unconscious incompetence through to unconscious competence in selling. It is like learning to ride a bike. In the first stage, the person is unaware that they cannot cycle, while at the unconscious competence stage, they cycle without thinking about the skills they have learned through trial and error.

This book focuses on the POWER© coaching model which stands for **P**urpose, **O**bjectives, **W**hat is happening now?, **E**mpowering, and **R**eview. Using the techniques suggested, sales managers and salespeople will be able to increase the successes they have with their teams. To stop learning is to stop living. The most important thing we can do as managers is to encourage others to keep learning. To do that, managers and coaches have to lead by example. The worst anyone can do is to assume they have heard it all before. Yet the most common barrier to increased ability is usually the existence of restricted vision and a closed mind. Coaching is not another one-year-only panacea. A major problem with many development programmes is that they are constantly shifting direction, depending on the whims of the incumbent chief executive or sales training manager. Coaching is an integral part of a whole development programme — but for a change, one that works.

If you want coaching to work, then you will also have to decide that you will stick with it until you and your team get it right. Coaching challenges you to change the habits of a lifetime, to adopt new concepts, new ways of dealing with old situations. It can take years, rather than weeks or months, to embed itself properly. Is that a bad thing? A long-term approach to coaching displays to the troops your commitment to making something work. That philosophy unfortunately does not fit in with Western business culture. We tend to work to shorter timescales. Some companies cannot see further than the quarter-end figures, and then they wonder why no planning takes place. It is important that everybody in the company understands the longevity of your coaching plans and philosophy.

The seed of greatness exists for all those who say they can, and even within those who say they cannot. Coaching can release that seed, not just for the person being coached, but also for the coach. This book can change your performance for the better. It has represented for the authors in their different professional applications a model upon which personal performance issues are clearly defined, structured and acted upon. It can do the same for you and for the people you seek to develop. It is the missing piece of the development jigsaw. Coaching offers a roadmap in the long journey to discover a better way of managing, training and developing salespeople.

# Chapter 2

# Salespeople Who Win

*"Everything in Life is Selling"* — Robert Louis Stevenson

**Basic Belief About Potential**

Essential to the effective practice of sales coaching is the belief that everyone has a wealth of untapped ability and potential. However, if you don't believe that people can perform better than they do currently, then you're probably right — they won't. That untapped potential may be a consequence of past management behaviour, or something which is self-inflicted. It could be that the potential may never be released (there are no guarantees), but it's there, and the best way to release it is through coaching.

If we are to explore what sales coaching is, then we must also explore what selling is. Therefore in this chapter we will look at what sort of material you have to work with — the salesperson.

**Looking for the Natural-Born Sales Wonder**

It is every sales manager's dream to have a team of top salespeople, but born salespeople seem very hard to find. How can you identify and attract successful salespeople to your company? How can you keep them happy? Is there such a thing as "the natural-born sales wonder" in your business, and if so, what are his or her attributes?

There are a number of chosen professions that may rely heavily on a particular physical attribute of some form or another but can we honestly believe that before birth some people are destined to be doctors, accountants, musicians, footballers, lawyers, actors, traffic wardens, managers, or salespeople? If this were the case, then Eric Clapton and Madonna could have been born in the middle of a Brazilian jungle but still been playing to packed audiences in the local hut; Roy Keane could have been born in an igloo in Alaska but would be the highest paid Eskimo in the English Premier division. It's about as unlikely as being born a salesperson.

## What Makes a Successful Salesperson?

We have been researching the area of successful attributes for many years to see if there are any distinctive personality traits or demographic profiles which predispose certain individuals to be successful in selling. Clearly many companies believe that "the natural-born sales wonder" exists. Why else are huge resources put into administering and interpreting personality questionnaires in the recruitment and selection process? Our research set about testing whether there were natural attributes which were consistently associated with success.

Starting at the most obvious traits, ones that can be ascertained from a CV, the research examined a number of demographic factors in salespeople — successful and unsuccessful ones — to see if there were any factors relating to gender, age or education which consistently pointed to success or failure.

### Gender

Our research[1] found that while men and women fail and succeed in equal percentages, women tend to be clustered at the

---

[1] Frank Salisbury, *The Effectiveness of Sales Training*, MPhil research, Oxford Brookes University, 1990.

top and bottom end of many sales forces, leading to a belief that they either succeed or fail dramatically. Most men, it seems, occupy the middle ground, with a few being highly successful. There are obviously exceptions, notably in financial services where the vast majority of salespeople who fail are men — mainly due to the fact that financial services direct sales forces are predominantly male. In many financial services companies, as many as 80 per cent of salespeople aren't achieving target at any one time, and labour turnover runs on average at 60 per cent. Even in non-financial sales forces, some 55 per cent of people are not achieving target and labour turnover runs at 40 per cent.

## Age

Age would appear to be insignificant: successful salespeople can be found across all age groups. The only determining factor about age with salespeople is that the older they are the less they are willing to change, but then this attitude is not exclusive to sales. They can change. They can learn new skills. They choose not to.

## Education

Whether salespeople hold qualifications or not appears to make little or no difference to their sales success. They may well be assessed as being more competent than those without qualifications, but the effect that competence has on sales success is not proven. The only way in which qualifications can enhance success in sales is in the confidence that it can give to the salesperson. Unfortunately, too many salespeople with qualifications believe that the customer should be impressed by their qualifications. They aren't.

## Experience and a Successful Track Record

According to our research, sales experience is not a strong indicator of future sales success. Experienced salespeople fail or succeed in equal numbers. This would suggest that companies are unwise to place too strong an emphasis on experience in a recruitment drive. It certainly helps if a candidate has in-depth industry knowledge or is already familiar with the customer base, but it doesn't guarantee them sales success.

In fact, trainees with no sales experience generally fare better than experienced salespeople in the short term. It isn't so much that "you can't teach an old dog new tricks"; it's just that the old dog doesn't want to learn any new tricks.

Success does not transfer well from one company to another. A person who is successful in one company may not be able to repeat that success in a new environment. The flipside of this is that failing in one company doesn't mean that the salesperson will fail in a different company. Indeed, we found that the experience of failure, for both salespeople and for sales managers, was usually a spur to doing well in the future. Salespeople do have a tendency to learn from their mistakes and failures. Unfortunately for most companies, the salesperson usually applies that learning elsewhere.

## Personality

Guion[2] has said that not only do sales roles differ but the personality characteristics required also vary greatly. This area of personality and recruitment is fraught with difficulties. Although a whole industry has grown up over the last 20 years supporting the theory that there is such a thing as a sales personality, we have doubts about the validity of the claims being made. Indeed, the scales of available research literature weigh heavily in favour of nurture as opposed to nature. In addition, we believe that placing the onus on salespeople to have a particular personality somehow releases managers from the accountability of developing salespeople. People often use the word "personality" on its own when what they really mean is a pleasing personality or a positive attitude. We all have a personality, for better or worse!

---

[2] R.M. Guion, *Personnel Testing*, McGraw-Hill, Maidenhead, 1965.

*There is no Identikit*

It is clear from the available research that it isn't possible to seek out specific "winner" personality characteristics or demographic profiles. Our findings indicate very strongly that there is no such thing as a successful salesperson identikit. This doesn't seem very helpful to the sales manager who is under pressure to put together a high-performing team. However, there are certain behaviours which can be associated consistently with successful people, just as there are negative behaviours that are found among unsuccessful people.

## Successful Behavioural Patterns

For us, an exploration of the behaviours displayed by salespeople has turned out to reveal more about success and failure than either personality or demographic features. A definite profile emerged of the top 20 per cent of salespeople who were enjoying significantly more sales success than the remaining 80 per cent. The research revealed a stark contrast between successful salespeople and unsuccessful salespeople. Successful salespeople:

- Displayed more energy
- Showed more initiative in finding business
- Displayed more confidence in their ability
- Appeared to believe in what they were selling
- Were fiercely loyal towards the company
- Had a purpose in life and set clear goals with deadlines for achievement.

Yet most importantly, and this would be consistent among all top performers in all professions:

- They accepted personal responsibility for their success and for any failures.

In addition, it was found that successful salespeople displayed more:

- Self-knowledge

- Knowledge of product benefits

- Knowledge of internal contacts who could help them

- Desire to be in selling

- Respect for the customer.

An important factor that separates top performing salespeople from the rest is their attitude towards the customer. They know that they will only continue to be successful by helping other people get what they want. Successful salespeople are customer-focused rather than sales-focused; employ low-pressure sales processes rather than high-pressure selling techniques; understand the difference between "I win and you win" and "I win and you lose"; and would rather say "the customer bought" than "I sold".

In addition — strange to say — top performers are also insecure. Seemingly, most don't know why they are performing at a high level, apart from hard work, and they're worried that whatever it is they have may one day be lost.

Nothing new, you might say. Yet these could be described as behaviours, especially when contrasted with the negative profile that emerged. The research found that those who were failing were the type who:

- Instead of accepting responsibility for finding business waited for the company to provide them with leads

- Constantly made excuses about their performance, blaming it on the recession, the product, the organisation or their manager

- Hid from contact with the manager and their peer group

- Displayed a negative attitude towards the company.

You might hold the view that these salespeople were like this because of their failure, not that these behaviours caused their failure. The argument is not relevant. Once in the trap, few rarely emerge. What you have here, though, are two sets of behaviours that can be used to create a greater level of self-awareness regarding your own behaviour and that of your salespeople. As a sales coach you need to support and encourage positive behaviours and help to change negative ones.

## Knowledge

Knowledge, it is said, forms the basis of a salesperson's career. Without knowledge of the company's products, the market available, and the role of the company in that market, a salesperson may be placed at a disadvantage by customers' questions about the product, a situation that could ultimately result in missed sales opportunities.

Salespeople need product knowledge to give them additional confidence, and the more they know the more confident they should be. High levels of product knowledge, however, like high academic qualifications, are no guarantee of sales success. Those with qualifications and/or high competency levels in terms of product knowledge are no more or less successful than those without.

There is a paradox about product knowledge. A salesperson should be an expert, but you have no need to prove to the customer that you are an expert by confusing them, or by droning on about your wealth of knowledge. The great French philosopher Voltaire once said that the best way to become boring is to say everything! Thus the maxim for the salesperson in terms of product knowledge must be: 'Know lots but talk little.' You cannot know too much about your products, but you can talk too much about them.

A high level of product knowledge may also make salespeople more confident, but confident about what? Many apparently confident salespeople fall to pieces in the face of a difficult customer or at the thought of cold telephoning. Their confidence is related to product knowledge and not to selling. In many organisations more time is spent drumming knowledge into people rather than skills. To what end? If a company's product is dynamic and keeps changing, then knowledge has a short shelf life, whereas skill can always be on the increase. If a salesperson were to spend as much time on skill acquisition as on knowledge accumulation, there would be a dramatic improvement in sales performance. It is far more important to find out what the product can *become* in the eyes of the customer than what it is.

### Skills

Too many people believe that skills are acquired on a training course. All a training course can ever do is to make you aware of the need to learn a skill. The acquisition of a skill takes considerably longer than any company can afford to allow you to stay in a classroom.

Watching someone else sell can look deceptively easy, as sitting next to someone else who is skilled at driving is deceptive. It looks easy because they make it look easy. The same would be true of a sport such as snooker. It looks easy enough on television. When you first try and play it, however, you realise almost immediately how difficult it is. When you are sitting next to someone who is driving you could be forgiven for saying to yourself, "I could do that. It looks simple enough, and anyway, if *they* can do it I'm sure I could."

The next step in the model (see Figure 1) is where you move to some awareness of your low skill. For example, suppose you try driving for the first time. For most of us, we will have been told how to start the car. Most of us will completely ignore the instruction and either stall the car or nearly burn the starter motor out in our keenness to show our level of competence, which at this stage is non-existent.

*Figure 1*

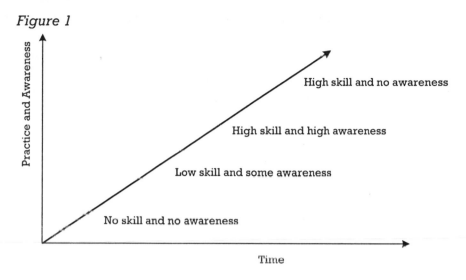

Driving, athletics, acting, music and dancing are all skills-based. You can't learn these things from discussion, books or watching someone else do them. They are activities you have to experience, something you have to do. They are physical skills.

Selling is a physical skill. It can't be learned from discussion; it is something you have to experience, something you have to "do". It is only through practising the skill that we can become aware of the potential length of the journey. Practice and failure makes us aware of where we are, like learning to drive. When you first get behind the wheel of the car you realise how much there is to learn. The same principle should apply to selling. Yet in most cases salespeople, sales managers and sales trainers fail to understand the analogy.

In selling, we use physical skills: speech, tone, words, eye movements, facial expressions, body movements. We can also use touch (handshakes and pats, etc.). But because these are learned at such an early age, we forget the process we went through to acquire the skill of communication. In this way, there comes a time when we stop learning. By practising a skill, we move up the model to the level of high skill and high awareness. We do things in a deliberate way to bring about a physical performance. We know how to do it, but it hasn't become innate enough yet to stop thinking about it all the time we are doing it. To reach this level of competence takes a lot of practice. Think about your driving test. You're exhibiting a level of high skill, sufficient to pass your test, yet it can be and usually is tiring.

Carrying out a physical task and thinking about all of the movements associated with that task is hard work. It can be exhausting. Depress the clutch at the same time as easing off the accelerator. Check the mirror while keeping an eye on your speed. Switch the indicator on whilst looking at your wing mirror and the traffic ahead. Practice, practice and more practice will ensure you have high skills and low awareness, as it becomes second nature to you. Once you have passed your driving test you quickly become a competent driver without thinking about all the stages necessary to start the car. And so it is with selling.

There are, of course, psychological issues to consider about practice and working hard. If you refer to Figure 2, you will see a visual explanation of what we mean. Over a period of time, we settle at a level of performance that we feel comfortable with (point A). This level could be high, low, or average, but the fact is we have great difficulty in moving significantly beyond that performance without some form of intervention by someone else, be that a manager, a trainer, or a colleague. For many salespeople it usually involves moving to another company and starting off fresh (and most salespeople up to the age of 40 do so every three or four years). However, many could be as successful as their aspirations in their present company, if only they practised their sales skills more often.

The difficulty arises when that practice begins. If we have been performing at a particular level (A) for some considerable time, then a training event (at point B) is more likely to have an adverse effect on our performance. Trying to improve someone's skills requires change and, as we know, change is not comfortable at any time, never mind change that involves learning to do something differently. It works well enough on training courses, but the vast majority of skills taught on formal training courses rarely alter behaviour on the job.

*Figure 2*

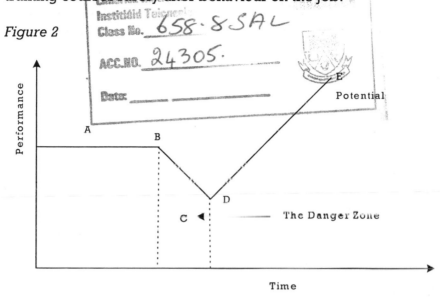

The reason for this is that learning to enhance your performance or learning to do things differently requires a significant amount of practice. During this period, it's quite common for performance levels to drop (point D). If you play golf, you may understand the principle. Most amateur golfers play off a certain handicap score for years without seeing any dramatic movement in their handicap figure. Once in a while, they might be motivated to take a lesson from the golf club professional. Inevitably the coaching given will result in the golfer having to change a particular facet of their play. They might have to stand differently, hold their club differently, or alter the height of their swing. Whatever it is, both during practice and eventual play, the golfer will experience a drop in performance. When this happens to a professional golfer, they continue with the practice until such time as the new or enhanced skill is mastered, eventually realising a higher overall performance level (point E).

The critical period for amateurs and many salespeople is during period C — which we call the Danger Zone. It's where things aren't going well and they give up, returning to their previous performance level (A). For all of us, learning involves a process of improvement, setbacks and plateaux. Professionals understand this; amateurs are fazed by it. Remember the adage: "An amateur practises until he gets it right; a professional practises until he never gets it wrong." Tiger Woods is a classic example of a true professional. He makes it look easy, which belies the amount of practice he puts into the game — both physical and mental. Woods may have played the game numerous times in his head whilst walking the course before the game actually starts.

Professionalism for Tiger Woods, in common with all professionals, is arrived at through a combination of knowledge, skills and attitude. In selling, many salespeople seek to achieve professionalism only through knowledge, whilst others rely on innate sociability. They fall into two distinct categories (Figure 3): the competent technician who is a sales disaster and the sales genius who is a technical incompetent.

*Figure 3*

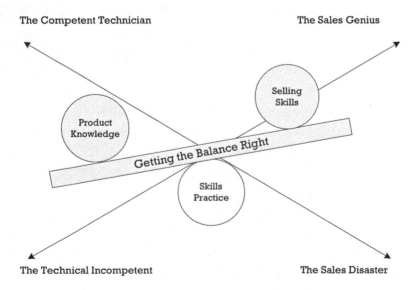

The former group are those who are extremely knowledgeable but poor at communication, while the latter group are great communicators but lack knowledge. Clearly there are others who appear to balance both, but they are and remain in a minority. The most common solution is to balance that difference through sales training. But that doesn't necessarily deliver new skills. Quite simply, salespeople need to practise skills, commonly known in other professional circles as skills drilling.

Perhaps the most dangerous combination is a successful salesperson with the associated traits of ego drive, empathy, and good social skills, but poor product knowledge. What this eventually produces are technical incompetents who can sell well enough, but are dangerous in that their lack of product knowledge and over reliance on the need to succeed can have them selling products to your customers which may be totally unsuitable. Eventually, the customers vote with their feet.

## Attitude

Let us suppose that the sales job has been identified as requiring the skills of listening, questioning and presenting.

Is listening a skill or an attitude? Do people have poor listening skills because of a lack of training or a lack of interest? Is listening a matter of poor attitude or poor hearing? Are people bad at asking questions because they don't know how, or do they lack the motivation to find out about other people? Is presenting simply a matter of acquiring the skill to do so? What about people who are terrified to make presentations to groups of people (which has generally been found to be the case for most of us)? Is the manner in which people communicate a matter of training or of conditioning, and if the latter is true, can that be defined as being part of our personality make-up or attitude? What is skill? Is it an innate ability that you are born with? Can anybody acquire any sort of skill? If most skills can be identified as being substantially influenced by attitude, can they be changed or enhanced?

It is certain that we can all, barring physical disability, already perform most of the skills that we are being asked to perform in a sales role. That is to say, we can physically perform those skills, given time, practice and feedback. So what stops us?

When we asked a number of sales managers this question about their salespeople, they came up with the following reasons:

- Wrong person for the job

- Bad attitude

- Not motivated

- Useless

- I didn't pick them.

The last response is known as the "inheritance factor". You will also notice that "attitude" appears again.

So if it's all about attitude, what can you do about it? Some people will say that you can't change attitude, but we believe you can. Festinger[3] has shown that by changing behaviour, attitude changes are also possible. Obviously it takes a long time, but then so does learning any new skill or changing firmly held beliefs. By changing behaviour, a cognitive dissonance is created which is only relieved by changing attitudes to suit the new behaviour. People are not born with an attitude; they acquire one through beliefs and feelings and experiences throughout their lives, and in this way attitude can be a dynamic entity. As we get older, however, we take on board fewer attitude-changing beliefs, as we harden ourselves to the pain of change. Attitude can best be described by referring to Figure 4. Our background, our life experiences, and the past behaviours we see and adopt, together with the knowledge and be-

---

[3] L. Festinger, "Behavioural support for opinion change", *Public Opinion Quarterly*, Vol. 28, 1964.

liefs we collect, determine our current behaviour and hence our current attitude. Our attitude will be changed by an increasing self-awareness, which produces a new behaviour, leads to new experiences, and develops into a new attitude. Mark Twain is reported to have said that when he was 16 he was dismayed by his father, whom he reasoned to be probably the stupidest man in the world. Years later, he said, "By the time I became 21 I was amazed how much my father had learned!"

*Figure 4*

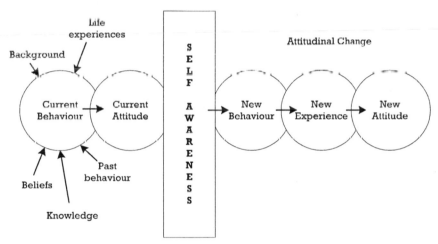

A good example of changed behaviour leading to changed attitude would be those people who say, "When we have children, we're determined that it won't change our lives." Those of us who have children know how wrong that premise and that attitude is. Whether we like it or not or try to resist it, the effect of having children, watching them grow, and feeling responsible for them makes an enormous difference to our lives. With hindsight, we wouldn't say, "It won't change our lives." The fact is, the adoption of new behaviours gives us new values, feelings, and attitudes.

Acquiring self-awareness isn't easy, but it is essential as a foundation stone for effective salespeople and indeed for coaches. Lasting change, and the self-awareness that sparks it,

requires help. The most obvious choice is your coach. By helping the performer become more aware and by encouraging
new behaviours, the coach can provide the spur to help you
gain the sort of attitude that winners need.

Some successful salespeople might say that there's no need
for further change or improvement — "I'm already a top performer, why should I need to improve?" However, if you continue doing things the way you have always done them in the
past, is that enough? Is that enough when, for example, next
year's sales targets are increased, or something changes in the
business environment? Even the best can and want to improve
their performance. A coach can help provide the impetus for
improvement through an initial process of helping the salesperson become more self-aware.

Defining the right attitude is a complex issue. We often hear
about having a positive mental attitude in sales and we would
go along with the theory that positive people tend to be more
successful at selling than negative people. It does, however,
remain a theory. There are plenty of miserable salespeople
who appear to be successful. However, attitude counts more
than either knowledge or skills in isolation. A person with the
right attitude will succeed in any case, but having both knowledge and skills will rarely work without the right attitude. Yet
attitude has sometimes been confused with behaviour, and displaying a positive attitude could perhaps be just as effective as
actually possessing one.

Perhaps salespeople need the sort of attitude that makes
them want to learn more about their current attitudes and the
way in which their behaviour affects others. Unfortunately, this
desire to open the Pandora's box rarely exists. Salespeople
tend to be narcissistic and interested in examining their personality characteristics, but they soon become sceptical when
adverse feedback is given, and seldom want to examine or
have others observe their negative behaviour. To give an example: when a certain salesperson was given some honest
feedback about his behaviour, this was his reply: "My behav-

iour has made me very successful in the past, and will continue to make me successful in the future. Are you suggesting that I will fail?" His coach said, "No. However, if I were to show that by modifying your behaviour you will be ten per cent more successful than you have been in the past, that would be helpful, wouldn't it?" He agreed. However, he failed to recognise a sale being made in the coach's question and his agreement. He subsequently failed to seize the opportunity to learn new skills, and ultimately failed in the job. It wasn't enough just to continue to do things the way he had always done them in the past.

## What's In It For Me (WIIFM)?

Let us suppose that a salesperson is identified as having a negative attitude. How can this be changed to a positive attitude? That's the sixty-four thousand dollar question that all companies are seeking the answer to. On the one hand, through perseverance a coach or a manager can force behavioural change, which in theory will bring about attitudinal change, but most managers find it difficult to gauge whether an individual salesperson has accepted the need for attitudinal change or is merely feigning acceptance. From the salesperson's viewpoint, it's tempting simply to agree to improve either your behaviour or attitude when faced by a manager whom you knew was not prepared to help you identify the root cause of your poor performance, but who simply wanted instant action from you. And herein lies the crux of the problem. Change of attitude can take an inordinate amount of time. Unless the salesperson tunes in to the WIIFM channel it won't happen. It becomes even more difficult if it's something you attempt to do yourself without the skills of a professional coach.

A coach can help those who want to change and improve to do so, which brings us to the final point about attitudinal change. You have to want to. You have to want to *change* your behaviour, not just simply improve. Everyone would like to improve their performance, but wanting to change is a less desirable goal for most people. Your current behaviour delivers your current results. All top performers accept that it is their behaviour that delivers their current results. Therefore, in order to change your results for the better you have to change your behaviour. This doesn't happen on training courses; it happens after the training course.

In a training environment, it's possible to motivate people to accept the need to change their behaviour in order to achieve improvement. But that motivation will last only as long as nothing happens to break the spell after the training event — such as breathing! It might last for a day or an hour. However, that hour may be just enough to make someone want to do something about changing instead of just thinking about doing something. For it to work, however, you have to already have decided that it's time you did something different. For many people and organisations, this is a paradigm shift in thinking. A paradigm shift involves seeing things in a different way. The new paradigm sees a sales training course as help on the journey of change where, for example, you might initiate the process of greater self-awareness through 360° appraisal behaviour. You see your behaviour in the mirror but also benefit from feedback from your manager, and possibly your team and customers as well. But even this intervention is not enough for most. The new paradigm sees the coach helping you to draw up a realistic action plan, which you own and want to follow up on for improvement in your performance.

## Barriers to Performance

In coaching salespeople towards improved performance, there are certain barriers which we have identified through research, workshops, and observation as common to salespeople in all types of industries and at all levels of experience:

1.  Low confidence and self-image

2.  A low sense of personal responsibility for their performance

3.  A low acceptance level of the need to practise selling skills.

Where many people make the mistake is in assuming that they can solve their overall sales force performance needs by employing people with the opposite of these characteristics.

Only 15 to 20 per cent of salespeople are highly successful and the stark fact is that merely because people are successful elsewhere does not guarantee that they will be successful with you. The reason for this is that your management style may not be conducive to creating and retaining high performers.

Between 80 and 85 per cent of salespeople appear unable to overcome these barriers. If you should manage to attract salespeople who represent the other 15 to 20 per cent of top performers, you still have no guarantees that they'll be as good or better in your team. You need to create an atmosphere in which they continue to feel self-confident, responsible and committed to continued learning about their products and how to sell them. Otherwise, you may either lose your high performers as they leave to seek a more challenging environment, or their performance may start to slide.

Most salespeople, whilst enjoying the perceived freedom and benefits of selling, exhibit internal conflicts which can dramatically affect their self-image, thus reducing their confidence. This in turn is transmitted to customers, bringing about a self-fulfilling prophecy of low performance. The beliefs which produce these internal conflicts include:

a) Few choose selling as a first career choice. Most people drift into sales as other professional careers disappear through lack of opportunity or qualifications. If we consider that those in other professions tend to have made a more determined choice early on (some as early as primary school days), then is it any wonder that salespeople might be handicapped before they even begin? Indeed, choosing a career at an early stage has a distinct advantage. The majority of lawyers and doctors will have received messages from their parents and educators about the need for application and commitment long before becoming qualified. But who is saying to young students, "Apply yourself well and you might be able to make a career in selling"? Messages about self-worth and preferred career paths start early. We quickly learn that the term "professional" is applied to a management cadre that excludes selling.

b) The route to professional status for salespeople is to become a sales manager. Many believe that sales management does not require any high academic achievement and that promotion to management is almost always based on sales achievement. Many salespeople are able to produce short-term performance levels in order to retire into management. For many salespeople, promotion is a reward for selling, rather than an acknowledgement that they possess the knowledge and managerial skills required to create an environment which encourages high performance among their sales team. Therefore, many sales managers find it hard to manage their sales team effectively and are ill-prepared to realise the potential in their team.

c) Salespeople and customers have the same feelings about selling in that the process is focused on benefits to the person selling, not the person being sold to. Although many sales training theorists talk about creating an environment in which customers are encouraged to buy rather than having to be sold to, the way in which salespeople are trained, managed and rewarded rarely allows this to happen. We can all too easily recount stories of instances where service provided by an organisation falls far short of the customer mission statements contained in their advertising. This can lead to mis-selling with negative repercussions. In this way, whilst salespeople are usually trained to match their customers' needs to the company's products, messages about targets raise feelings of significant conflict once they are in the field and subject to the usual sales management pressure of achievement.

## So What is the Answer?

The answer to professional sales success and how to coach salespeople doesn't lie in the sort of training needs analysis hitherto prevalent in most sales forces. We believe that the complicated sales training analyses and sales management practices currently being conducted in many companies are wasteful and ineffective. What is certain is that the plethora of solutions being offered to find, train, and develop "the natural-born sales wonder" are being sold effectively, otherwise why would so many companies be buying those solutions, and why are there so many consultancies offering them? Yet here we are peddling our own solution. The difference, we hope, is that this solution is based upon common sense, 30 years of research, and is simple to apply, although we accept that it isn't a quick fix, either in its learning or application.

## Successful Behaviours

By the summer of 1999, having analysed thousands of sales calls over a period of ten years, what emerged was a set of behaviours which we believe have a positive influence on the outcome of the sales process, and ones which the sales coach can help the performer to learn and improve upon (see Figure 5). You will see, however, that we have identified much of this behaviour to be attitudinally based, and that the single most important influence on this attitude is the behaviour and intervention of the coach.

*Figure 5*

**Successful Behaviours**

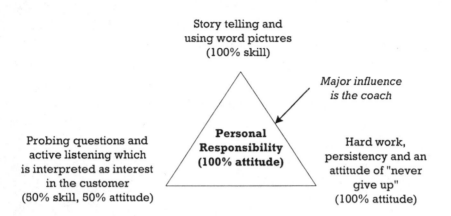

Story telling and
using word pictures
(100% skill)

*Major influence
is the coach*

Probing questions and
active listening which
is interpreted as interest
in the customer
(50% skill, 50% attitude)

**Personal
Responsibility
(100% attitude)**

Hard work,
persistency and an
attitude of "never
give up"
(100% attitude)

## Story Telling and Using Word Pictures

Having witnessed thousands of salespeople, we see a distinct difference between those performing at a high level and the rest. It took some time to analyse this difference, but eventually we realised that the conversational style used by high achievers differed significantly from their lower-performing peers. Whether it be in selling or in any other field, most of us have a predilection for wanting to listen to high achievers. It's not so much that they tell us about their achievements, but they phrase their conversation in such a way that makes us want to listen. You will have heard of using word pictures, but how many people actually do it? Yet learning by pictures and story telling is the essence of the way in which we acquire information today. Consider television or the Internet. Both are primarily picture-oriented with a storyline underpinning each. In time, the Internet will also deliver the readily acceptable and preferred method of learning through pictures with a narrator providing an audible dialogue. Top salespeople display both sets of stimuli regularly. It's something which looks innate, but it can be learned. Remember, top salespeople have learned the behaviour themselves. They may have a head start because of background or experience, but nevertheless, as a coach you can help other salespeople acquire the same ability.

## Probing Questions and Active Listening

An effective salesperson needs the ability to probe for information from the customer and to actively listen to the response. The former produces relevant information aligned to the customer's individual needs and the latter allows the salesperson to match products and services with those needs, or at the very least know when to sell and when to stay quiet. Where the latter point is concerned, however, whether the salesperson does ask the right questions or bothers to listen to the answers is based upon attitude. Why else have questioning and listening been consistently identified as skills necessary for successful selling? Yet so many salespeople appear unable to do so. It isn't because they can't — it can be learned — it's because they don't have sufficient motivation to do so. They haven't found enough right answers to the WIIFM question — what's in it for me? It's no good simply saying, "Well, that's your job", without additionally providing them with a motivational reward for having done that job.

We would also caution you against the traditional training method of separating "open" questions from "closed" questions. We don't believe that simply asking "how", "what", "why", "when", "who" and "where" brings about open conversation, no more so than "do you want this?" brings about a closed response. In exactly the same way that the vast majority of techniques for overcoming objections and closing don't work, simply learning words isn't enough. You have to sound as though you mean it.

You can teach people to remember the phrase, "I didn't tell him to steal your purse", yet each time a change of emphasis from one word to another will completely change the meaning. For example:

- *I* didn't tell him to steal your purse (meaning it was someone else)

- I didn't *tell* him to steal your purse (meaning I might have intimated it but I didn't actually tell him)

- I didn't tell him to *steal* your purse (meaning I might have told him to borrow it or hide it, but not actually steal it)

- I didn't tell him to steal *your* purse (meaning I told him to steal someone else's)

- I didn't tell him to steal your *purse* (meaning I told him to steal something else.)

Straightforward enough, you might say, yet how many people practise vocalising the difference? It's something that you as the coach can force people to do. Practice can then help the salesperson make their presentation more effective.

One thing is certain: asking people the right sort of questions in the right sort of way draws people's attention and invites their trust and interest in you. By showing interest in others, they will reciprocate. This is the way for the salesperson with their customer as it is for the coach with their performer.

*Hard Work, Persistency and Never Giving Up*

Ask any high achiever what the reason for their success is and you will undoubtedly hear "hard work" as a main response. The American baseball player Maurice "Mo" Vaughan put it succinctly: "I have seen hard work beat good luck seven days a week." However, hard work on its own still isn't enough. Top salespeople rarely admit that they have a formula, but if you spend as much time observing top salespeople as we do, you'll see a formula emerge. We have already said that they tell stories, use pictures and ask questions that show interest in the customer. They work hard, and yet research has shown that top salespeople see fewer customers than lower-performing salespeople, making a lie out of the myth "see more people". Besides preparing themselves more than their lower-performing peers, they give that bit extra by trying again and again. Top performers don't give up easily. They don't pester the customer; they just keep on going and building the relationship until eventually the customer buys. It would not be unusual to hear a top performer say, "I've been after this account for three years. I think I'm nearly there." Lower performers give up easily, becoming discouraged at the rejection. Yet many salespeople bring about rejection themselves. What we have observed is that top salespeople don't back customers into a corner by asking them for a decision, no matter what. This doesn't mean that they ask open questions rather than closed questions. They appear more sensitive to the customer's indecisiveness by accepting personal responsibility for the customer's lack of commitment.

**Personal Responsibility**

We mentioned personal responsibility at the beginning of this chapter and it bears repeating at the end. It is the keystone to success and high achievement in all walks of life. It is something we will cover in more detail in Chapter Four. However, for now you should accept that the major influence on a salesperson's behaviour of accepting personal responsibility is the coach.

There is no evidence to support the theory that there are specific personalities more suited to sales than others. Salespeople are not born, they are made. Selling is not a matter of knowing the right techniques and tricks, and good salespeople can't sell everything. The influence on each is the environment. As a coach, you're responsible for the environment you create for the salesperson. We observe that only 15–20 per cent of salespeople possess the attributes of a successful salesperson. The mistake is to believe that you can find and hire that small percentage. The problem is that most selection methods won't allow you to identify "the natural-born sales wonder", because it isn't possible to pick out specific "winner" traits: success doesn't depend on gender, age, experience or personality.

Success is an outcome of behaviour. Most salespeople display low levels of confidence, personal responsibility, and the need to practise selling skills.

But there is no such thing as an all-rounder — it only exists as an average. None of us is average. Our attributes are balanced by our disabilities. To become better at selling, focus on people's attributes. In doing so their disabilities will be crowded out. Coaching is the key to helping sales managers unlock the potential in *all* their salespeople. Sales managers who embrace coaching can make a big difference in the performance of their people. Part of your job as a coach is to weigh up the total package: the attributes and disabilities. Make a call with regard to accepting people's failings compared to their attributes. When we spoke recently to Brian Kerr, an integral member of the Irish soccer coaching squad, he agreed. While encouraging and nurturing the performer's attributes, you'll also have to make a call with regard to their weaknesses. Are these failings development needs? Will the performer want to address them? Will these weaknesses adversely impact your sales team? In a soccer context, Brian Kerr, one of Ireland's most successful coaches, pointed out that sometimes you have to accommodate the player who doesn't conform: "If you let an eccentric star go because they aren't following the rules, and you haven't tried to harness their talents and manage them, you run the risk of them haunting you as they may go on to perform to a higher standard for the opposition." The difficulty will always be in ensuring that the disruptive nature of non-conforming stars doesn't damage the equilibrium of the whole team, but then all too often sales managers are obsessed with creating a team atmosphere in an environment where everyone is judged on the same targets, not on their contribution to the team's efforts.

# Chapter 3

# Taking a Professional Approach

*"A competent professional listens well, probes, asks questions, and thinks before he speaks. This is easy to say, but hard to do."*
— *Jeffrey G. Allen*

**What is Professionalism?**

When Allen said the above in 1998 he was talking about business in general. He could have been talking about selling. In the previous chapter, we said that good salespeople ask probing questions and they show they are listening. We also pointed out that good salespeople work hard. Allen was right: acquiring the habit of both is not easy, but then it has been said that nothing that is any good comes about easily.

Much has been said about professionalism in selling and yet we already know that almost no one chooses selling as a career. When we are running workshops or seminars on the subject of selling, we often begin by asking people to write down what they wanted to be when they were at school. The room fills up with would-be doctors, solicitors, accountants, nurses, artists, footballers, and a thousand other occupations — except selling. In 20 years of research, we have identified less than one per cent of people who chose sales as a career. This fact alone is a major stumbling block in selling. People don't want to be in selling and therefore don't treat it as a profession.

We've been on numerous sales training courses where the trainers attempt to ingratiate themselves with the trainees by saying something like, "Your job is not different, is no less professional than, say, a doctor, or an accountant or a lawyer." Let's get one thing straight — for 99.9 per cent of people currently in selling, it could not be further removed from those professions. For one thing, there's no need to study; for another, there are no formal qualifications you must have before you can take up your profession. (This is beginning to change in financial services as a result of legislative compliance requirements.) There is no apprenticeship and there are no recognised standards. Even though there have been significant moves over the last few years to improve the image and professionalism of salespeople — notably by the Sales Institute in Ireland and the Professional Sales Institute in the UK — selling as a profession on this side of Western Europe remains a doubtful career choice for your sons and daughters.

However, in most companies salespeople are the single most important link with the customer. For many customers, the salesperson *is* the company. Yet within those same companies, being a salesperson is rarely seen as a worthwhile career. The commonly held belief is that if you have talent then it might be wasted in sales.

## Selling is a Physical Skill

Selling is not a profession in the true sense. There are professionals who practise selling. In the same way, some would argue that sports is not a profession, but there are professional sportspeople. Apart from classical music, music itself may not be classed as a profession but there are professional musicians. Apart from ballet, dance in general may not be a profession yet there are professional dancers. Strangely, acting is seen as a profession. We say "strangely" because actors become professional in very much the same way as sportspeople, dancers, and musicians, and yet appear to have more kudos than these counterparts.

As already noted in Chapter 2, selling is a physical skill. There are some soft issues included, but the crux of a professional approach should be focused on those aspects that are in common with professionals such as sportspeople and athletes, musicians, actors and dancers. The dedication of these professionals is mainly exemplified through hard work and practice, something that's in short supply in selling. However, if we were to begin by berating salespeople for their lack of commitment and hard work, we would be met with a tirade of, "Oh no, not me. I work very hard. I put long hours in", etc. etc. Putting in long hours and working hard to what end?

Why mention these professionals in the same terms as selling? It's because we believe that selling is the same. It is a physical skill and mastery of that skill through similar methodologies used by sportspeople, dancers, musicians, and actors will and does bring about professionalism.

## Career Choice Dictates a Professional Approach

There's also another important factor to consider about these professions. Earlier we mentioned that less than one per cent of people choose selling as a career. If you ask the people in the professions of sport, music, dance or acting, what they wanted to be when they left school, 99 per cent will say, "What I am now." In many cases, someone else will have fuelled their desire at a very early age. It could be a parent, grandparent, guardian, teacher or any number of role models. It won't be something they were born to do, it will be something they grew into, although the desire will have been developed and fashioned whilst they were more aware of their possibilities than their shortcomings. It is only later that we acquire doubts about our abilities. As children, we believe anything is possible.

The fact that these professionals have chosen a particular path in their lives gives them a significant edge over salespeople who haven't. The former are more open to the rigours of the professional processes which we describe below. They are less suspicious of teachers (managers, trainers, and coaches) than

salespeople are. They are better team players — they understand that more can be achieved by working together with
other people. They focus on the positive, not the negative —
they think about success, not about failure. There are more dif-
ferences than similarities with salespeople, unfortunately, so
the fact is that the raw material you're dealing with is often less
than perfect. We're often asked by prospective coaches how to
cope with salespeople who don't fit the perfect mould. The
plain truth of it is that you simply have to work harder at
coaching than your professional coaching counterparts have to,
but then the satisfaction of achievement will be all the greater!

Further into the book, we will explain how to create a vision
for the team and for your individual salespeople, which is to replace the lack of professional vision with which most will have
entered the profession. For now, let's explore some basic processes which should lay the foundation stone both for your understanding and for that of your sales team.

### Professional Processes

So what are these processes? Figure 6 shows a model entitled
"Professional Processes" which suggests the elements that
many professionals need to adopt in seeking to acquire and
display top performance. We firmly believe that if salespeople
understood, accepted and adopted these principles, they
would deliver higher performance levels than they have hitherto. In addition, if you, as the coach, followed the basic principles that are laid out here, you would be taking the first
significant step in releasing the power of your sales teams.

*Figure 6*

**Professional Processes**

## The Rules

The model begins with rules. True professionalism comes from a starting point of accepting the rules within which the professional can perform.

In tennis, you might have heard John McEnroe complain about the ball being in or out, but not of the necessity to serve over the net. In football, players try to get away with infringements of the rules, but they know that they can expect to be cautioned, sent off, and even fined and banned for repeated fouls. All sportspeople know what the rules of the game are before beginning to play.

In music, Nigel Kennedy may have complained about always playing "dead guys' stuff" but he doesn't change the notes of the music or leave parts out when he does play it. Musicians understand and accept that there are rules to music, one of which is that you play in tune. I can be the greatest guitarist in the world, but if I start playing in a different key to the rest of the band, I'll soon be playing solo to empty seats. From jazz to traditional music, there are rules that must be followed by performers to avoid a cacophony.

Your job as a coach is to determine the rules that apply to your sales process and to have all the players (your salespeople) understand that their job is first and foremost to accept the rules, and then to apply them.

For example, in Chapter 2 we proposed that successful salespeople tell stories. If you believe that this is an integral part of your sales process that people should use, then either provide them with the stories or insist they develop storylines that you agree with before meeting a customer.

If you believe that using word pictures or actual visuals will enhance your company's sales messages, then you should insist that pictures are used on every client call. You may also insist that they are of a certain quality. If you spend fortunes developing visuals, then they should be used. All too often when we visit companies we see cupboards full of brochures and presentations that someone has developed but nobody uses. When we ask the salespeople in that company why the visuals aren't being used, they say that they're no good.

Picture this: I'm a player in a football team. The football league introduces a new ball. It's green and it's lighter than the one I'm used to playing with. I don't like it. What happens? I end up using it because that's my job. My job isn't to design footballs. My job is to kick them to the best of my ability within the rules I've accepted. I'm a professional.

Your first job as coach is to identify and explain the rules of the sales game for you and your company. If the rules are too flexible, then you can't coach. Think about the sales process as being contained within a total professional game. For example, if you were to view the arena in which the professional game of selling is to be played as similar to that of a tennis court, you might be able to visualise how the game would begin.

For example, there's an opening (stimulus) and from that stimulus you hope to achieve a particular response. Therefore you want to place that stimulus in a certain sector of the customer's court. Obviously in this game there have to be two winners, but the principles of serving your opening and receiving a positive response don't infringe the rules of win-win. Your next step is to determine how you actually want the opening served. Is there something you specifically want the player to say? Is there something you specifically want the player to use to illustrate the story they have to tell? Is there a structure to the sales process that you want the salesperson to follow?

The salesperson's job is to follow the rules to the best of their ability, not to question them. Your job is to lay out the rules clearly so that everyone understands what's expected of them. The sooner you do this the better. The best time is during the selection process, so that there's no misunderstanding when people start playing the game for you.

The sort of rules that might apply to your salespeople could include such things as:

- Practising — you might insist that your salespeople have to practise their basic openings at least once a day.

- Implementation of policies, compliance and regulatory processes — in some industries, e.g. financial services, the way in which the salesperson acts and conducts the sales process is highly regulated. You should insist that they observe the rules in this area at all times.

- Being observed — as a coach you cannot determine how to help people improve if you don't observe them at work. They have to understand and accept that this will happen regularly.

- Learning what "good" looks like and copying it — if you have determined what "good" looks like, then your sales team has to learn how to replicate it.

- Consistency — you can insist that they be able to deliver a basic performance to a basic level of competence whenever asked to do so.

- Show the customer that we're listening — the salesperson has to be able to learn and deliver a performance which is based on active listening techniques.

- A structured approach to the sales process — you may decide that you want the sales process to follow a certain structure based on, for example, best practice. It's your right to demand that this is adhered to.

- Understanding, accepting, and acting on the vision — as part of your vision, you may decide that you want to operate in a particular market, or that you expect certain ethical standards. Your sales team is therefore required to follow these aims.

## Basic Training

In order to release talent and ability, people have to be able to learn and perform the basics, mostly through repetition and skill drilling. The important thing is for you to be able to say with certainty what it is that make up the basics.

When we have watched professional coaches in other disciplines, they seem to have no problems in deciding what's involved in basic training. When we watch sales coaches, it's another story altogether. You must work out what is basic and what is advanced. Basic is what you expect people to be able to do and achieve as a basic minimum. You need to be able to decide how realistic it is.

For example, as a football coach I want to see that you can kick the ball in the desired direction. I don't expect to have to show you how to do that. My scout will watch you play before I make a move to have you join my team. As a professional sportsperson, you will expect to be watched playing and to undertake a medical before joining a club.

So why are so many salespeople offered jobs simply by attending interviews? Despite research showing that reliance upon interviewing as a means of determining job ability is as scientific as throwing darts at a list of names, many companies still use interviewing as a predictor of job ability and of potential success in the job.

We believe the reason for this is that many companies and sales managers have no confidence in their ability to identify what the basics of the job are. It is a prerequisite of sales performance coaching that you are able to identify the minimum standards required and to audition prospective candidates who wish to join your sales team to ensure that they can perform the basics. This is based on the premise that there are sufficient people in the employment pool that can display the basics — which is no guarantee.

Too few sales managers have confidence in demanding to see a basic level of performance before coaching people to excel. You can't coach people without seeing them perform the basics, which as we have previously explained means that you too have to understand what the basics are. Remember, it is your game and they are your rules, and if people want to play in your team then they have to play by the rules and be able to show you that they can perform the basics.

Basics for salespeople might include:

- Sales selection interviews — ensure at a minimum that the job applicants go through a sales simulation exercise. For example, if they are required to sell home loans, you could ask them to sell you a loan in a structured role-play. In this way, you'll be able to observe their sales strengths and weaknesses upfront.

- Skills drills at sales meetings — instead of passing on information or doing tasks that could be done by e-mail, fax or post, you should insist that the team practise their sales skills at each and every meeting.

- Practise — it's something that every professional except salespeople do. Your job as coach is to instil a practice regime, whether your salespeople want it or not. We already know they don't practise enough, which is why only 15 to 20 per cent of salespeople are currently exceeding target. There is no other profession where you are allowed to practise on a live audience other than as a salesperson or a sales manager.

- Structure and scripts for customer approaches and sales situations — make sure that the individuals in the team can adhere to a structure at any time. A good time to check it out is just before a sales call — assuming you go on calls regularly with them.

- Warm up — every professional returns to basics just before a performance. We hear about the need to return to basics as though it was something unusual. Make it the norm by instructing your salespeople to warm up before every customer meeting.

*Warming Up*

The more you warm up, the less chance there is of injury when you are performing. All professionals warm up. Professionalism is not just about being paid to do something, although it's important to understand that if you are paid to provide a certain performance then you should do so in a professional manner.

Before salespeople give a presentation, they should warm up, whether that presentation is at a conference, to a businessman in his office, or to a customer at home. We usually associate warming up with giving a presentation at a conference, although we have seen far too many presenters walk on stage without warming up.

Warming up should involve the physical process of selling. That means speaking the words aloud and if possible also making the actions that accompany selling, especially the opening. It is no good just thinking about what they want to say and do. To be truly effective and to give them the confidence they need, they should say the words aloud and accompany the words with the body language they intend to use. That's not to say that mental rehearsal has no place — it's an important factor in its own context. Many top professionals use mental rehearsal immediately before the performance when physical rehearsal is not appropriate; for example, it's pointless rehearsing a 100-metre run seconds before actually doing it. Some sportspeople (such as Jack Nicklaus) in particular would say that mental rehearsal could be a 50 per cent contributing factor to their success. It has been shown that mental rehearsal can stimulate physical processes and it helps us to see ourselves winning.

When professionals practise, they use the same skills and physical processes in practice that they do when delivering the actual performance. To deliver a performance of high quality they have to believe that they're performing in front of others each time they practise.

We have observed that many salespeople have a great reluctance to use role-play. In most professions, practice plays a large part in developing skills and is the key to excellence in performance. In selling, however, salespeople steadfastly resist practising their skills. This resistance to using role-play may also account for the high failure rate among salespeople. It seems that salespeople get their practice in real sales situations. In order to be successful, salespeople require a high self-image. It would appear that displaying inadequacies in front of their colleagues is either embarrassing or an indication of weakness. Salespeople are unlikely to rate highly any course that concentrates too much on role-play, and yet as professional trainers we know that it is role-play that determines how effectively trainees learn a new skill.

Remember that skills can only be learned through repetition and practice. It's only by practising something that we become aware of the potential length of the journey towards excellence.

Practice and failure makes us aware of where we are. You may be disappointed if you fail but you won't get off the starting block if you don't try.

We learn skills through repeating them and our confidence and competence will grow. If you are learning selling skills, either you go on the same course again and again or you could do something about it yourself. One goal won't win you the golden boot. One composition won't make you into another Paul McCartney. One story in the local paper won't herald you as the next Frederick Forsyth. The gap between simple ability and continuous performance is wide and deep and it relies on repetition. It's easier to turn in an average performance than to go for excellence. There is a direct correlation between practice and level of skill achievement. Don't we remember our parents or mentors exhorting us in our youth that practice makes perfect, or, if at first you don't succeed, try, try and try again? Unfortunately, common sense isn't always common practice in sales.

Does that mean that you have to aim for perfection for yourself and your salespeople? Certainly not, unless you define perfection as trying to be the best you can be. Perfection, by our definition, is not attainable. That isn't to say that some people fool themselves into believing that they have achieved it. Whether they admit it or not is another matter. There are those people who ease into a comfortable performance — they stay in their comfort zone and, in performance terms, stand still. Standing still and delivering the same performance may be acceptable in their organisation. In fact, the "standing still syndrome" is quite usual in top performers. For many people, performing at a level above colleagues is what it's all about — "So long as I can keep a step ahead, that's all I want."

As we said earlier, however, the people performing at a high level also have great feelings of insecurity. Being out in front is just as stressful as being way behind. In many ways, being out in front can be more stressful. In their minds there's only one way to go — down. At least the person at the bottom, having hit bottom, can say that the only way now is up. In a lot of ways, coaches have more difficulty getting top performers to increase their skills, ability and performance than they have with low performers, and yet the same process and rules apply.

## Use of Tools

Most professionals have tools that they use and they also understand that the way in which those tools are used requires compliance with basic rules. An actor knows that they have to use a stage prop in a certain way at a certain time, and they know that they have to stick to the script. A dancer uses a certain type of footwear specific to a particular dance style. They accept that they have to perform a number of steps in a certain sequence. A guitarist knows that they have to strike the strings of a guitar in a particular fashion and hold the strings on the fret board in a certain way in order to comply with the music — which they follow.

The tools of selling might include such items as:

- Sales reports — these allow the salesperson to determine their current level of performance in relation to where the sales manager wants them to perform.

- Training packages — salespeople can use these to return to basics.

- Sales presenters, visuals, brochures, and point-of-sale systems — they have to be used in a certain way. For example, you don't simply give a brochure to a customer to read, you take them through it, highlighting the important points you want to make. If using a particular point-of-sale system (e.g. a presentation constructed on a laptop computer) you might want to ensure that the customer sits in a certain place whilst you present.

- Development journals — does each salesperson in your team have a personal development plan? If not, then it's time they did. Where do you record what training has been given, how the trainee has reacted to that training and what they have learned?

## The Desire to Improve and the Role of the Coach

Once performers have experienced the benefits of practice and structure, and eventually the release of talent and personality, it becomes a natural development to reach for constant improvement. Yet it's not that easy — there's a missing element.

Whenever we ask senior managers the reason for one team performing well and one not so well, the answer is inevitably the manager. Our own experience and research over the last ten years bears this out.

The major influence on sales success is provided by the behaviour of sales managers, not salespeople. In common with other professional groups, changing the manager changes group performance for better or worse. It's the same with sport. Peter Ridsdale, Chairman of Leeds United, put it succinctly: "I have always said that in any football club, if you have only a limited spend, spend it on the best manager you can. Everything is down to the quality of the manager."[1]

Yet in most cases of poor sales performance, the first casualty is usually the salesperson. Even though you may have set the scene with regard to rules, basic training, the use of tools, and the need for consistency and inflexibility, you additionally need to understand that without the desire to improve, people will always deliver below their potential. The key to unlocking potential is the coach.

Professionals understand and welcome the involvement of the coach because they recognise that they won't achieve their potential without the intervention of a coach. Whenever top performers are asked to comment on their success, inevitably they refer to the coach. For example, in the Heineken European Rugby Championship in 2000, the Munster rugby team were rank outsiders but stunned everyone by reaching the final.

---

[1] *The Irish Times*, 26 August 2000.

Team members all alluded to the influence of the coach, Declan Kidney, when reflecting on their team's success.

We have observed hundreds of people performing their jobs, where it is possible to see how those with the desire to improve their physical delivery have in time improved the outcome of their job. Likewise, we have seen those with emotional barriers say things such as, "I've always done it this way. I can't do that. I can't say that." As a consequence, these people continue to deliver a poor performance and deliver less-than-acceptable results.

Your major message to your team has to be about the need for constant improvement. How you construct and transmit that message is covered in the next chapter.

# Chapter 4

# From Salesperson to
# Manager to Coach

*"Treat other people the way you would wish to be treated,
and never forget what it was like to be managed."*
— *Frank Salisbury*

### Behaviour Begets Behaviour

The way in which the salesperson feels about the job they do
has a major impact on their effectiveness, but that's not the
whole story. All sales managers are drawn from the population
of salespeople and therefore bring with them the same bag-
gage they acquired in their sales role. Although many want to
treat their old peer group in a different way, few have been
shown any other example other than the status quo of "there
are those that lead and those that follow". Indeed, most sales
managers take up their new positions without any instruction,
formal or informal. They then adopt the behaviours their past
managers have taught them, perpetuating the status quo.

Insofar as personal responsibility is concerned, we found
that most sales managers believe that they are responsible for
the success of their teams. Whilst they are certainly accountable, no one can be responsible for the performance of another
person. It is a difficult and complicated lesson to learn but it

represents the foundation stone of professional performance coaching. Figure 6 in Chapter 2 shows that the major influence in the attitude of personal responsibility needed for success is the coach. How you behave towards the salesperson will ultimately dictate how they feel about themselves.

Messages about self-worth, preferred career paths, and the nature of authority start early. We quickly learn that we generally have to do as we are told, that people in authority have the upper hand, and that the term "professional" is applied to white-collar work, excluding sales. In addition, the lessons about being personally responsible for decisions and success begin too late to have any effect.

By the time most people begin their first job, the way in which they relate to authority has become embedded. Unlearning these patterns of behaviour requires a significant effort on the part of both the employee and, especially, the manager. Remember, managers have themselves been subject to the same history. By the time they arrive in a management role, they have convinced themselves that their position of authority now bestows upon them the responsibility to change others, whereas as Argyris[1] rightly said in 1962:

> No one can develop anyone apart from himself. The door
> to development is unlocked from the inside.

## Management Influence

Each person is responsible for their own personal performance. Each person can become better at a particular skill *today* than they were yesterday. For many people, however, improvement goals are usually set for tomorrow: "I'll start that diet tomorrow . . . as soon as I get the exercise bike . . . after I come back from holiday . . . when I've finished this packet of cigarettes." Personal effectiveness and responsibility for per-

---

[1] Chris Argyris, *Interpersonal Competence and Organisational Effectiveness*, 1962.

formance improvement only really happens when dealt with within the immediate time-scale. In order to acquire, improve, or retain a skill, there has to be desire, commitment and determination to actually do something now.

What we have found is that managers find it difficult to associate with or understand why it is that so many of their salespeople appear not to have that same sense of responsibility that they themselves display. Yet we only observed it as a natural phenomenon in less than 20 per cent of the sales population anyway. Paradoxically, it is this 20 per cent that is "farmed" to produce the current sales management population. It would be akin to promoting all of your best football players in a team to be managers. There's a significant body of evidence in these professions to suggest that taking the best professional performer is no guarantee that they will make a good performing coach.

As you move from selling into sales management, you will no doubt be exposed to a great number of theories and purported effective practices of management. Each will be accompanied by a recipe for managerial success, rather than realising that the answer to sales management success lies within their current salespeople, not with quick fixes. The potential of salespeople can be compared to an iceberg, where we see their current level of performance as that which appears above the water, but their potential as something which sits beneath the surface and can only be realised through coaching (see Figure 7).

*Figure 7*

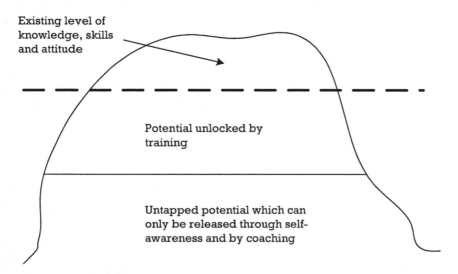

**The Performance Potential Iceberg**

Existing level of
knowledge, skills
and attitude

Potential unlocked by
training

Untapped potential which can
only be released through self-
awareness and by coaching

Despite this fact, there are as many sales managers failing each day as there are successful salespeople. As with sales success, there remains a constant search by trainers, managers, and the jobholders themselves for the secret of sales management success and apparently the money to pay for it. Enormous sums are spent yearly on management training and development, but recent surveys show that less than a third of top and middle managers feel that they learned anything important, whether the training was conducted within their own company or through outside courses and consultants. The figure for in-house training looks particularly bleak at fewer than ten per cent.

As we have already said, the vast majority of people we have met in selling didn't want to be salespeople when they were at school, college or university. For this reason, a large percentage, given the opportunity, opt to take sales management roles when the situation presents itself. For many, after a successful period in a front-line sales role, promotion to a sales manager's position is simply a mechanism to keep them in the company.

There is no guarantee that successful salespeople will be good sales managers but one thing we believe is certain is that managers have to be able to sell. We believe that there are three basic skills that sales managers have to possess to be successful:

1.  They have to be able to sell

2.  They have to be able to train

3.  They have to be able to motivate.

**Selling**

If you want to be successful in sales management, you have to know how to sell. You have to be able to get yourself in front of people and then make a sales presentation that will make people buy from you. The other factors like training and motivation revolve around the basic principle that the sales manager knows how to sell. At some stage the manager is going to have to show his or her people how to sell, thus you have to be successful at it. You don't have to be number one, but you have to be successful at it. For one week, sometime in your sales career, you must have made the target. You must have reached the minimum standard, and that's not easy. Then you will know what success is. You have to understand how good it feels to have done just that, to have sold something to someone. Then you can empathise with the salesperson. Empathy is important in selling and it's important in sales management.

We have looked at the areas of the job that salespeople find most difficult, and it's only through experiencing those difficulties that sales managers can empathise with them. For example, we already know that prospecting is the area in which most salespeople have their greatest problems. It is the area that invokes more nervous breakdowns, more stress and ultimately more failure than any other area. Yet in many industries, that's the reason for employing salespeople. It's part of their job to find people to sell to. You have to help them and boost their confidence to the extent that they not only know how to do it but also want to do it. You also have to understand that they don't want to do it. Who in their right mind wants to ring up total strangers just to be rejected? We've sat with people before and told them to ring somebody up, and they've said, "No, I can't." There are times where you have to make the call for them to show them how to do it, which is high risk for you, because you won't get 100 per cent success either.

We believe that you have to have some experience of selling to understand how people feel about this. There will be times when you have to pretend there will be no pain attached to the job and that you and your people are going to enjoy picking the phone up. In reality, the better you become, the more professional you become and the easier it will be for you and them.

## Training

Sales managers have to train. What works in sales training? The thing that works in sales training and what makes the difference is the trainer — not the package, not the content. It's the person who does the training that will determine the success or failure of a sales training programme. They have to have first-hand experience of the subject. If you haven't been in selling you aren't going to be a good sales trainer. If you haven't been in sales management, you're going to struggle in relating to trainee sales managers. You won't know what you're talking about, so you might just as well give trainees something to read for all the good it will do. The most effective sales trainer is not a staff trainer or a central or external resource, but the line manager responsible for the salesperson. The only person qualified to train salespeople in the field is the line manager. They've got the authority and they're the ones who are ultimately responsible for the development and success of their people.

If managers are generally promoted because of past performance levels, then it seems folly not to use their knowledge and skills to coach others to the same levels of high performance. Whilst this may seem obvious, many companies see coaching staff as a trainer's role and move managers into administrative functions for which most are ill suited.

Sales managers have to be sales trainers, which gives them credibility. Staff sales trainers don't have the same credibility, because people will say that if they could do it they would be doing it themselves. They also have to demonstrate it, which means field training. What frightens most sales managers is the fact that at some stage on some field visits a salesman will say, "Look, I can't get this right, show me how to do it." Salespeople see through sales managers who can't do the job and they have no respect for them. They would rather work for sales managers who know how to do the job and can, than for the manager who only knows the theory.

Surveys[2] into sales and management training clearly show a disappointing reality about the lack of effectiveness of sales training. The fact remains that most skills training doesn't last or make any impact on the bottom line. The need for training is widely recognised but the difficulties of making it measurably effective are great. The implication is that sales management aren't providing the right climate for creativity to flourish, and given the regularity with which new techniques in marketing and promotional methods appear, it will be increasingly necessary for sales managers to initiate programmes to stimulate their sales teams to adopt a more creative approach to the development of sales from their territories and accounts.

The simple reality is that, unless some management action is taken to prevent it from happening, new skills acquired in training deplete to vanishing point in a few short weeks unless the manager creates new tasks to provide the opportunity for the newly trained salesperson to use new skills.

---

[2] "The Sales Direction Survey of Sales Management", *Sales Direction Magazine/Management Exchange Ltd*, 1989.

## Motivating

What motivates salespeople is debatable. Is it possible to give people self-motivation? We believe that it is, although there are few people who can do it. It may sound strange to say that salespeople have to be motivated to want to succeed, but our experience shows that salespeople devote more energy to fear of failure than to the desire to succeed.

Success in selling is a mixture of external and internal factors. The external factors come with the job and include knowledge, experience and — more than anything else — the influence of the sales manager. Internal factors are those things that come from inside — self-motivation and the right attitude. You can't guarantee that all new starters will arrive with evidence of either on the surface, and it is the sales trainer's job to get trainees to dig deep within themselves and find the motivation that should be there.

In 1987, Kovach[3] produced a paper that examined the results of previous research into employee motivation. The factors swung from "the need for recognition" as the main motivator to "having interesting work to do". We favour the work carried out by Shipley and Keily[4] in the early 1980s, which shows that salespeople are motivated by reward, recognition and achievement.

Winer and Schiff's research in 1980[5] found that salespeople placed a high priority on financial reward as a main motivating factor in job performance. Making more money was specified as an important motivator. If reward is the primary motivating factor for salespeople, then you must link your training events with that by getting trainees to establish, early in the training

---

[3] K. Kovach, "What Motivates Employees?" *Business Horizons*, September 1987.
[4] D. Shipley and J. Keily, "Motivation and dissatisfaction of industrial salespeople", *European Journal of Marketing*, Vol. 22, No. 1, 1988.
[5] L. Winer and J.S. Schiff, "Industrial salespeople's views on motivation", *Industrial Marketing Management*, 1980.

event, what it is they want from the sales job. Your training should be seen as a method of obtaining just that.

The point of all this is that sales trainers and sales managers have a joint responsibility to motivate people to want to learn, but to do that, everyone needs to fully understand the problems presented by closed minds and negative attitudes. Somewhere along the line, in your role as a trainer and a sales manager, you have to create your own stories and analogies. They don't come out of books or exist in other people's training notes. They come from experience, and especially experience of having been there yourself. Good sales trainers and sales managers have a history of both success and failure, and are prepared to share those experiences, especially with new employees.

Most managers still find the subject of how to motivate salespeople a complete mystery. Levinson's article[6] on the subject is particularly revealing. He says that motivational theory is hardly sparse and most executives will have studied the subject in depth at some time or another:

> Many have taken part in managerial grid training, group dynamics laboratories, and seminars on the psychology of management, and a wide range of other forms of training. Some have run the full gamut of training experiences; others have embraced a variety of panaceas offered by quacks.

But like most skills training he believes that the expectations of companies that their people will change after a training event, no matter how senior they are, is totally unrealistic, and we could not agree more:

> Furthermore, it is one thing to become aware of one's feelings; it is quite another to do something different

---

[6] H. Levinson, "Asinine Attitudes towards Motivation", *Harvard Business Review*, Jan/Feb, 1973.

about managing them, let alone managing those forces that affect the feelings of other people. Experience is not enough; training in a conceptual framework and supervised skill practice is also required.

Sales managers need to be wary of adopting blanket motivational approaches, and concentrate more upon the individual.

### Managerial Behaviour

The important thing to consider is that people learn from how managers behave, not from what they say. When we facilitate training for managers, we usually conduct the following self-awareness exercise. We ask them to think about a manager for whom they used to work who they would describe as a poor manager, then to consider what it was that manager did, said, and how they behaved that made them a poor manager, and lastly how it made them feel. The responses we have received include that the manager was:

- Never there

- Unapproachable

- Patronising

- Apathetic

- Selfish

- Uncommunicative

- Unpredictable

- Inconsistent

- Always telling lies

- Only interested in results

- A bully

- A sexist.

We then ask them to describe a good manager for whom they have worked. The responses include that the manager:

- Listened
- Had time for me
- Showed empathy
- Asked my opinion
- Encouraged me
- Gave both freedom and responsibility
- Kept commitments
- Gave firm guidelines and expectations
- Was approachable
- Created a good team atmosphere
- Rewarded with praise and with money
- Believed in me — I had no limits.

Unfortunately, there appear to be more poor managers than good managers and we tend to learn more from poor managers than from good ones, the reason being that poor management is easier to execute. It takes less time. Being a good manager is difficult: it requires hard work. Our contention is that good coaching equates with good management.

## Moving from Sales Management to Sales Coaching

Much of sales management is an instructive process. This is extremely important for groups such as new starters. Although there are many theories of motivation, one important theory — Douglas McGregor's Theory X and Theory Y[7] — forms the foundation stone of sales performance coaching.

---

[7] D. McGregor, *The Human Side of Enterprise*, McGraw-Hill, 1960.

The basic principle of performance improvement is that each and every one of us has the seed of greatness as a right. For some it gets watered early on, nurtured and cared for until the seed becomes strong and self-reliant. For others the seed is neglected, stunted and appears to have withered, but the seed remains. It might not grow to its original potential, but it still can grow. Dependent upon our environment, some achieve their potential easily; for others it can be a struggle; while for some it never happens.

The manager as coach has to have complete belief in the potential of individuals, with the proviso that the potential of those individuals is limited to the performer's desire, commitment, and physical possibility. It is said that we only use a fraction of the skills we are born with, in the same way that we utilise a mere fragment of the potential of our brains.

It could be that you've heard this before and might even have said it at some time, but somewhere along the road the high aspirations you had for people didn't materialise. Perhaps they let you down, perhaps you let yourself down, or perhaps it was just bad luck. Perhaps the theory didn't turn into practice and all the role-play in the world didn't prepare you for the real world. The latest fad was just that — a fad.

There are bound to have been times when you returned from a management training course full of ideas and ideals, keen to try them out on the troops. Some of those ideas never got off the ground, and others, well, you can at least say, "I tried that once and it didn't work."

In the meantime, life goes on, people come and go. You have successes and failures and either you make it to the top, settle somewhere round the middle, or have already sunk into obscurity. And the effect you have on other people? Who knows? How many come back and tell you?

Yet there is a way for you to get what you want by helping others get what they want, and the mechanism allows both parties to feel good about the process. The process is sales performance coaching, but what does it mean?

## Coaching is not Training

For most people, the term "coaching" has merely replaced the word "training" as a means of teaching or instructing people. Already, many trainers and managers talk about their coaching programmes when what they really mean is their training courses. Someone once said, "You train animals — you coach people", and while this is extreme there is some truth in it.

Training is about teaching people to do the basic job. It can be good for trainees, but for most managers with any semblance of intelligence, it's boring. People are trained to do a job in a particular way; they can be coached to do it better. The Pareto principle — that 80 per cent of successful production comes from 20 per cent of the workforce — is a result of the assumption that people reach the limit of their ability. By that we mean that people reach the limit of their ability to be trained. Coaching helps people to enter a zone as yet untapped.

That untapped zone exists in "The Performance Potential Iceberg" (Figure 7). We all come to work with an existing level of knowledge, skills and attitudes. Training releases a further level, but for most people a significant mass of knowledge, skills and the attitudes that lead to successful performance remain untapped.

## Personal Responsibility

As referred to in Chapter 2, inherent in the philosophy of coaching is personal ownership and responsibility. Recent research has found that managers who suffered from stress, when pressed, realised that the stress was a result of their feeling that they lacked control. They accepted their own management responsibility, but found it difficult to accept the blame for poor performance of subordinates when they had tried extremely hard to help poor performers to improve.

An example from the athletic world is that, having coached an individual to a record-breaking time in practice, and subsequently the same record-breaking time was delivered on the track, how responsible should the coach be if another athlete delivered a faster time? Obviously, what other people do cannot be dictated — perhaps planned for, but not dictated, and certainly not coached for. Also, what personal responsibility could the coach have if the athlete tripped during the race? Obviously none. Let's look at an example. In the Melbourne Olympics, Alan Storey, coach to Sonia O'Sullivan, summed it up well when referring to her preparation for the big race:

> All I can do is put Sonia on the starting line as fit as it's possible for her to be and then hope she runs the race as quickly and as cleverly as she can. She'll finish first or second or third, but if she doesn't it won't be because she wasn't properly prepared. It will be because there are better people in the race.

Sonia came second in the 5,000 metres. It wasn't as good as first but it was better than thousands of other hopefuls. The coach did all he could. Sonia took personal responsibility for her own performance.

What about in a work environment? If a person has been coached to deliver a performance in a negotiation situation, and someone else delivers a better performance, what personal responsibility should the coach shoulder? The same answer applies — none. However, in business, as in sport, the coach may ultimately be *accountable*. In sport, the coach may not take their team to the Olympics. In business, the coach may be beaten at the negotiation table and subsequently the firm may suffer. That accountability goes with the job. The problem is that many managers confuse responsibility with accountability. Responsibility is a personal thing and can only be attached to those things over which you have direct control.

Sometimes, for the best of reasons, most times because it is easier and quicker, managers take on board the personal responsibility of completing a task, either by telling people specifically what to do, or by doing part of or the whole task themselves. It is normal when the manager is absent for the task to be completed to a greater level of efficiency by the team, who enjoy the freedom to express themselves without interference.

## The Traditional Role

Traditionally, managers are seen as focusing on end results. The traditional model for management could be represented by Figure 8, in which managers seek to push people from their current performance to the company's desired performance levels. The focus for both manager and subordinate is usually the desired performance. In many organisations, desired performance is considerably higher than current performance. Inherent in this continual focus on target is failure.

*Figure 8*

**Traditional Management Practice**

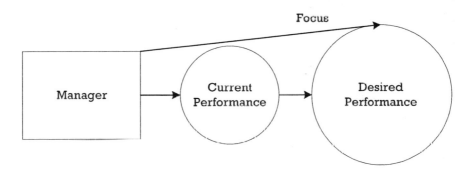

Many recent surveys show that people at work are unclear as to the company's objectives and where they fit in. Target setting is usually an arbitrary process, having already been decided some time before any manager–subordinate discussion takes place. Managers have a tendency, which is reinforced by management training, to regard forecasting and objective-setting as their remit, and whether operating in a democratic fashion or not, will only occasionally involve subordinates in the process, by which time it is often too late to make any difference.

The fact is, left to their own devices and given the right environment (a true coaching environment), people can and have been known to set themselves far more demanding targets and goals than the manager would have done.

There is another way to manage. Doing it differently and acting as coach can potentially produce significantly higher performance levels than any other form of management. It can reduce levels of stress in management and produce, for everybody, the sort of working environment that has not as yet been seen in most organisations. Other benefits of adopting a coaching style of management are that:

- A better relationship is formed between managers and employees

- The working environment is less stressful to both

- The focus for many people moves from promotion to improved job performance.

The greatest difficulty you will have as a manager is resisting the desire to take control of the individuals in your sales team. Changing the attitudes of people who have been in sales management for some time is certainly the most arduous job we have. It begins with a need to make sales managers aware of the effect that their behaviour has on others. There are three phases that all managers have to go through:

1. Self-awareness — understanding what it is like to be managed;

2. Letting go — releasing the potential that others have — you don't have all the answers;

3. The need to empower people with the responsibility for their own actions.

**Phase One: Self-awareness**

At Phase One, we have to learn about ourselves and need to have an awareness of our true interaction with others. The process of self-awareness is a painful one. The rewards, however, could be enormous, but for many of us the thought of letting go is terrifying. It would be like saying to someone who is frightened of water to jump in the deep end: "Don't worry — you'll be all right. It's the only way to learn!"

For many sales managers, the transformation from manager to coach can smack too much of social work. It sounds like personnel and training theory. Some of us will quickly assume that this is yet another "flavour of the month" training fad and that's the problem — the boy cried wolf once too often. The response could be: "Over the last decade we have been faced with one theory after another, and this is just another one, only worse. In this one we are being told to let go — to stop focusing on targets, to abdicate performance responsibility, to give up controlling people. It's a veritable nightmare."

That's why going through the phases is important. You have to understand what motivates you personally, what makes you tick, and why you were so keen to get into management in the first place. For many, the main motivation for promotion was to give up the current job, for whatever reason. For sales managers it could be a case of, "Selling's a great game so long as someone else is doing it!"

The tragedy of it is that when many managers get the opportunity to change the lot of their previous peers, the stress, the boredom, and the lack of opportunity and growth are soon forgotten. For other managers, one of the main reasons is to get away from the person who is their manager, to get away from being told what to do, and to be in charge — primarily of their own time.

This is important. People don't like being told what to do. Some sales managers fool themselves that they democratically agree targets with their subordinates. They forget how they felt when the same game was played with them. There is no such thing as negotiating targets. The manager always knows what's required. If the subordinate starts off low, the conversation continues until the agreed target is at least at the low end of what the manager wanted anyway. The manager and the subordinate know this. If the subordinate's offer is high, either the manager says nothing, grudgingly accepting it, or pretends to negotiate, nearly fainting with excitement as the figure goes higher and higher. And the result? Most people don't achieve their target. A further 20 per cent exceed their target by a sufficient amount to cover those that don't meet theirs, and everybody is happy until the next time.

Throughout all of this pantomime, sales managers continue to look concerned most of the time as they struggle to find a way to cope. None of the theory works, none of the courses help, not one of their peers has any better ideas other than to "keep them focused on the target".

There is another way to manage. Doing it differently and acting as coach can potentially produce significantly higher performance levels than any other form of management. It can produce the sort of working environment for everybody that encourages confidence rather than conflict.

The main function of a coach is to develop people's potential. Companies do have a need for managers in the traditional sense, but we would advocate that their skills might not be in the area of people management. It is indeed rare to find people who have excellent administrative *and* excellent people skills, and yet we seem continually to assume that in management they exist.

### Phase Two: Letting Go

Phase Two involves the manager letting go. They have to give up controlling people, being responsible for individual performance, and imposing target performances. Nobody likes being controlled. The coach can't be responsible for the performance of the individual. Yet, as already noted, the coach may ultimately be accountable.

If the individual fails to deliver their potential performance on the day, and yet in practice appeared capable of doing so and was seen to be capable of doing so, then the coach can't be responsible for that failure. Yet many managers assume personal failure in the failure of their subordinates, as though it were possible to shoulder blame just because they hold the manager position. It's a fine balance. There are also managers who refuse to accept their accountability. A coach needs to provide the resources and support to enable an individual to take responsibility for their own performance. The sales coach must:

- Provide the individual with sufficient support when it was needed

- Reach full agreement on areas of personal responsibility

- Provide the individual with sufficient feedback in order to determine the true likelihood of executing the task.

*Figure 9*

**New Model of Manager as Coach**

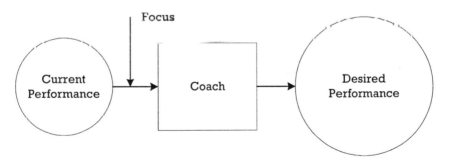

**Phase Three: Empowerment**

Most sales managers make the mistake of trying to solve all the performance problems of a salesperson in one session. Coaches know that this is impossible. Empowerment doesn't mean abdication, and it certainly doesn't involve setting unrealistic improvement goals. Our performances are made up of parts. The skill is in being able to describe those parts in detail so that they can be broken down into skill sets that can be worked on. By focusing on one part of the total performance and working on it to make it bigger when that part is put back into the whole, the performance will increase. It's a simple enough principle, yet easily missed by both performers and managers. In this way the new style of manager as coach is about taking the first step towards performance improvement — pulling the performer towards the goal rather than pushing. The performer finds this approach easier to deal with. It's impossible to improve everything all in one go. We can only cope with one thing at a time when it comes to improvement. By focusing on one step at a time, the performer will move forward towards the goal. The other major benefit of this process is that the performer will constantly re-set the goal, moving it further away and therefore ultimately achieving far more than would previously have been the case.

# Chapter 5

# What Does it Take to be a Good Coach?

*"Always bear in mind that your own resolution to
succeed is more important than any other one thing."*
*— Abraham Lincoln*

### From Selling to Coaching

There are some widely held beliefs about sales coaching that
we would like to expose, namely:

1. *Manipulation and sales coaching are the same thing.* This is
   not true. Professional sales coaches are able to get people
   to work for them in ways not necessarily for their own good.
   However, they also help salespeople recognise areas of
   mutual interest that can produce benefits for both parties.

2. *Giving it your best shot is all that really counts.* This is not
   true. Too many people substitute effort for accomplishment.
   The reason for the sales function and the sales coaching
   function is to get results. You can help salespeople to work
   smarter, not harder, but the bottom line is what really matters. Working hard is not enough.

3. *Empowerment is the same as delegation.* This is not true.
   Delegation is telling someone what you want when you want

it and how it's to be done. Empowerment is about helping salespeople to understand, through your behaviour, that they are responsible for their own action and that it's those actions that bring about results, good or bad.

4. *Sales coaches have to come from the ranks of top salespeople.* This is not true. A sales coach is not a person who can do the work better than others, but is someone who can get others to do the work better than they can.

5. *Sales coaches must control all situations.* This is not true. Tight control mechanisms restrict personal responsibility in salespeople.

## Looking in the Mirror

At the end of this chapter you will find one of those question-naires that people seem so interested in completing. We in-clude it with tongues in cheeks. On one level, it may help you to determine how good you are; on another it may encourage you to try harder. The chances are, however, it will have little effect. We maintain that self-awareness, or looking at your behaviour in the mirror, is a critical element of performance improvement, whether you are a salesperson or a sales coach. The problem is that, given the choice to become aware of our shortcomings, we all tend to choose self-analysis rather than critical feedback from someone else — and self-analysis is far from accurate. As John Hillier, the CEO of the National Council for Vocational Qualifications, said at a conference a few years ago: "I can con-vince myself I am in control of my weight providing I don't go anywhere near the scales."

What happens is that we tend to protect ourselves from criti-cism by not putting ourselves in the position to be criticised. Most of us would say, "I don't mind criticism, providing it's ob-jective and not personal." The fact is that all criticism feels per-sonal, yet it has to be said that the only valid feedback is that which is given by someone else, someone who is qualified to do so. So far as salespeople are concerned, that means you, the coach. This means that, insofar as your salespeople are concerned, you have to sell the idea that they need feedback, and that the best feedback will be from observation. It is not enough to rely on the performance of the practice pitch to judge *real* performance. What happens on the practice pitch is only ever a rehearsal at best. The measure of any true performance happens on the pitch. At any rate, the questionnaire and the feedback on profile has been used by many managers we have met, who would all say that it has helped them to focus on changing their attitudes towards their perceived coaching ability. But then, they would say that, wouldn't they?

## Vision

Lincoln's statement, quoted at the start of this chapter, is true no matter what your calling is. We have already seen, however, that the existence of a resolution to succeed is not on the surface of everyone's "performance potential iceberg". It is probably there, but for many people it has to be unearthed. Who better than the coach to do this? Common to all successful teams, whether in sports or in sales, is a leader with vision, purpose, and a desire to achieve.

This book is not about goal setting, but setting goals does have a place in coaching. Whether the individuals in your team have already defined their goals or not, you need to consider what your own goals are and how you intend to influence the team in achieving them; you have to find a way of expressing your goals so that the individuals in your team adopt them, and your goals have to become their goals. If self-awareness is the first thing that a successful coach needs, then the second is a vision.

Every leader should have a vision of where it is they want to be. Every coach has to have a vision of what it is they are trying to achieve. You also need to be able to express it in such a way that influences others to invest emotional and physical time in achievement of your goal. You need to bring your vision to life and it should be something that you can constantly refer to.

Most of us will have a tale to tell about some teacher in our past who was responsible for either firing up our interest in a particular topic, or damping down our interest. Parents are sometimes astounded by children who appear to acquire an aptitude for a subject not previously on the family agenda. In some cases, the influence of the teacher will also have led directly to a particular career choice.

Before constructing your vision and the manner in which you want to communicate it, you need to be aware of the direction in which the company is going. Does your vision reflect the vision of the company? Having conducted this exercise on a number of occasions, we have found that in 99 per cent of cases, the sales message that the executive starts out with rarely reaches the customer (Figure 10), other than through advertising. The more layers of management there are, the more the message begins to be distorted, with the only consistent message from the top to the bottom of the organisation being achievement of target. This is clearly not customer-focused.

*Figure 10*

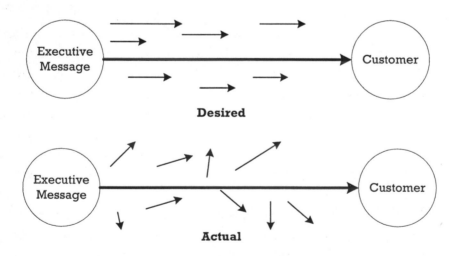

By the time the message reaches the sales force, the training department have constructed it into a process which, whilst promoting a particular way of selling in the classroom (if at all), is never followed up in the field. This in turn allows the salesperson to adopt whatever sales process they wish — which they do. Because communication is confused from the top to the bottom, most salespeople simply make it up as they go along. The top five to ten per cent have a formula for success which they use and know works but which they cannot describe. When asked to do so, they rely upon the same mythology as their lesser-performing peers.

Your vision statement should not just be about the journey; it should also contain messages about how you intend to get there. You need to find a way to explain how you intend to implement the professional processes referred to in Chapter 3. In addition, you have to find a way in which to bring your message to the attention of your sales team by employing the same methodologies you want them to employ with the customer; for example, story telling, word pictures, or personal experiences.

Your vision should inspire people and contain some examples of where you have overcome the odds in the past to succeed. It's no good expecting people to follow you if they think that either you have never achieved anything before or they get the impression that you are making it up as you go along.

You need to give your salespeople the impression that you will succeed, whether they are with you or not. Your commitment to success must be explicit. Whether people buy into your vision initially or not doesn't matter. What's important is that you believe in it and are seen to believe in it. You will find, as you consistently strive to achieve your vision, that people will join in.

It is also important to vocalise your vision. It's no good just writing it down and sending it around the troops. Too many company vision statements are plastered on the walls of organisations which have little or no meaning for the great mass of people working in those organisations. Tom Peters states that:

> Visions come from within as well as from outside. . . . Posters and wallet-sized cards declaring the vision and cor-

porate values may be helpful, but they may not be. In fact they can hinder and make a mockery of the process if the vision and values are merely proclaimed, but not lived convincingly.[1]

In a recent survey[2] 85 per cent of workers questioned expressed no confidence in the quality of the company's leadership or the vision they had been fed. Yet in the same survey, 90 per cent of those workers said they were committed to giving their best. The environment in many companies, however, works against the release of potential.

## Creating a Positive Environment

We are all products of our environment. In Chapter 3, we expressed the view that salespeople are not born, they are made. It is the environment that we work in that produces people who succeed or fail. You are the major influence in that environment. There may well be many things that are wrong in your company, yet it's a fact that the main influence on any worker is that person's line manager. This is nowhere so true than of salespeople and sales managers.

The environment can and does change everyone. It either reinforces what we believe and causes us to respond, or it takes us by surprise and produces an adverse reaction. We found a startling number of salespeople who had experienced the "when I started on Monday it wasn't the same company" phenomenon. We also found a correspondingly large number of sales managers who experienced the "when they started on Monday morning they weren't the same person I had interviewed" phenomenon.

The problem is that far too few recruitment and selection criteria are made on an examination of skills and behaviour, and far too many decisions are made on personality and interview alone. The environment that you create for your salespeo-

---

[1] Tom Peters, *Thriving On Chaos*, Macmillan, 1987.
[2] MORI Survey, *People Management*, 1 October 1998.

ple starts with the selection process. Besides testing the skills and behaviours you want to see in a salesperson, the selection process is where you lay out your expectations. You should make it clear what is expected of the new salesperson before they start, and what they can expect of you. For many professional coaches that we know, the expectation of success is a primary tool in the arsenal of success they have. We call it the self-fulfilling prophecy.

## The Self-fulfilling Prophecy — The Pygmalion Effect

Managers communicate their expectations of people in a number of ways, both verbal and non-verbal. Even managers who believe in the potential of their team and who say something positive about the work of their subordinates need to pay attention to the tone of their voice, their look, the general lack of concern shown in their body posture; otherwise, they can impart a totally different meaning to their team.

Managers can and often do communicate both negative and positive expectations to others by saying nothing. Giving employees the "silent treatment" or the "cold shoulder" tells people more about what the manager is really feeling than a load of meaningless words. It isn't what the manager says that counts, it's the way they behave.

What managers expect of employees and the way in which they treat them determines their performance. Low expectations bring about low results; high expectations bring about high results. Experiments conducted in the 1960s by people like James Sweeney, Professor of Industrial Management and Psychology at Tulane University, and J. Sterling Livingston, Harvard Professor of Business, confirm the existence of the Pygmalion Manager.

Some managers treat their employees in a manner that results in superior performance, whilst others treat their subordinates in a way that elicits poor performance. The unique characteristic of superior managers is that they have and transmit high performance expectations of their charges, which are fulfilled.

In study after study, encompassing such companies as Metropolitan Life Insurance Company, AT&T, West Coast Bank and the Texas State Employment and Education Agency, the existence of the Pygmalion effect was found. Managers were told that certain groups of employees had been tested and found to be of superior quality than others. In each case, the groups thus identified performed at significantly higher levels than the control groups. In reality, the groups had been picked at random. The only factor that led to increased performance was the way in which the manager treated the individuals in the identified groups.

In one particularly remarkable experiment, Robert Rosenthal and Lenore Jacobson told a number of teachers in a secondary school that following intelligence tests, 20 per cent of the children had been found to be intellectually superior to the others. Follow-up tests confirmed that the 20 per cent did in fact perform higher than the rest of the school.

The disturbing fact was that all 20 per cent were chosen at random, and that, when asked to rate the high achievers, the teachers said they were more attractive, appealing, and better adjusted than the rest.

Rosenthal identified four factors which he says influence the Pygmalion effect:

- **Climate**. Managers who create an encouraging social environment that includes warmth, attention, smiling, and appreciative non-verbal signals.

- **Feedback**. Managers who give more specific verbal messages about employees' performance, who give more sincere praise, and even criticism when appropriate — all of which assist the employees in improving their performance.

- **Input**. Managers who stretch employees by giving them more difficult tasks and help them to learn more.

- **Output**. Managers who encourage questions, allow staff time to develop, and give people the benefit of the doubt.

The people most affected by the Pygmalion effect are young workers and those new to the job. New people in particular are dramatically influenced by the way in which the manager treats them and introduces them to the workplace within the first few weeks of employment.

The characteristics displayed by Pygmalion managers and coaches are:

- They have belief in themselves and confidence in what they are doing.

- They have belief in their personal ability to select, train and motivate people. Even when they pick the wrong people they rarely give up in the attempt to improve them.

- They have an ability to communicate their positive expectations, which are both realistic and achievable, to their employees. Setting unrealistically high goals for employees only leaves workers dissatisfied and accepting far lower results than they would originally have achieved on their own.

- They have a belief that people can make their own decisions in life and at work. They encourage workers and empower them with the authority and responsibility for achievement.

- They prefer rewards which are a result of the achievement of their subordinates, not of their own achievements.

In our own surveys, when we have asked salespeople whether the job had matched up to their expectations, 65 per cent of people said it had not. The challenge is clear. Managers must learn to believe in themselves before they can inspire others to believe in them and, as Rosenthal says:

> We still do not exactly know how the Pygmalion effect works. But we know that often it does work, and that it has powers that can hinder as well as help the development of others.

More recent studies continue to highlight the all-important role played by the line manager in the relationship with their direct reports and their commitment to the company.

## Commitment

In the 1990s, the Gallup Organisation undertook large-scale research on employees' commitment to their companies. The research showed a strong relationship between employee commitment and productive outcomes, including productivity, profitability, and customer satisfaction and employee retention. It is not surprising to learn that an employee who is committed to the company is more productive and provides higher-quality customer care. The question is: how can you help your sales team to be more committed?

The Gallup research revealed that the relationship between employees and their first-line managers or supervisors was key to creating strong commitment towards the company and the job and in turn generating the four productive outcomes highlighted above. Good managers are prepared to put a lot of effort into creating positive relations with those they supervise. They set clear and reasonable goals, provide feedback, give praise and help their employees' growth and development.

A sales manager who acts as coach can create this positive learning environment. More important than any financial incentive, recognition and encouragement of individuals and teams will engender loyalty and commitment. Big targets won't create big results. Performance coaching breaks up a task into small steps and looks at how each individual's performance can be encouraged and improved so that longer-term targets can be reached and even surpassed.

## Questioning Skills

Coaching is essentially a questioning skill. In later chapters, we will outline key questions which will help you use the POWER coaching model. However, simply becoming better at questioning belies the atmosphere and environment needed to obtain right answers from the questions you ask. The difficulty is that, as a manager, you have the authority to ask questions of the salesperson. Similarly, the salesperson has a duty to answer the questions, but whether they do so willingly, openly and honestly is another matter.

Some people would have you believe that you have to ask open questions which encourage people to talk, as opposed to closed questions which cause people to answer yes or no. This sounds good in theory, yet in practice it may not happen.

Neuro-Linguistic Programming (NLP) exponents may be right to claim that the barriers to successful communication are our perceptions, emotions and past experiences. There are two fundamental elements to communication, namely *stimulus* (the information which is sent and therefore begins the communication event) and *response* (the way in which the information is received and the reply). On the surface, this appears straightforward. NLP practitioners believe that a potential barrier to effective communication could be the fact that you might not be offering the customer the information in their preferred format. They say that you should take time to test which media format the customer prefers to receive information in. Those three media are:

- Audio

- Visual

- Kinaesthetic.

The theory behind the third expression purports that kinaesthetic people prefer to deal with feelings, and that by focusing your questions on the other person's feelings (e.g. *How do you feel about that?*) the communication will be more open.

It is said that through observation, listening to responses and general analysis, we can arrive at the ideal medium that best suits the other person. This might work if you have a lot of time and a degree in psychology. For the rest of us, it is sufficient to realise that messages we send can be forgotten quite quickly by the receiver. In addition, it might not even arrive in the same format you wanted it to, simply because of the potential barriers that exist to communication. You may think your message has been conveyed accurately, but because of different perceptions, the recipient's understanding might be totally different, and they therefore respond unexpectedly. Words mean different things to different people. Remember how our example "I didn't tell him to steal your purse" can mean different things, depending on how the words are spoken (see Chapter 2)?

The recipient could have recently experienced an emotional upset. If they have something else on their mind whilst you are trying to coach them, you may believe that you have the solution to all of their performance problems, but you might not be getting an effective hearing.

*Effective Questioning*

To be "effective questions", they have to do two things: raise awareness and generate responsibility in the performer. Let's focus on these two areas and refer to the Bisham Abbey coaching team, where important lessons can be learnt.

Sir John Whitmore[3] describes how, during a golf coaching session, he asked a trainee to tell him whatever she noticed or felt when she first swung at the ball. He wanted her to focus her mind and to find out where her attention was focused. He then reflected her words back to her. This checks your understanding and lets the trainee explain further if necessary. He confirmed with her that she wanted to produce "a more fluid swing", and followed her interest. He didn't introduce his own agenda — she retained responsibility. He asked her to focus on her swing. He then helped her to narrow her focus and raised her awareness even further by first asking her to describe, on a scale of 1 to 10, how fluid her swing was, and then at what point she noticed any awkwardness. The whole process was then re-

---

[3] *Coaching to Improve Performance,* Training Video, Performance Consultants, London, 1998.

peated as the trainee focused on different aspects of her performance.

The coach asks questions in order to raise awareness within the performer, resulting in improved performance and then a sense of personal responsibility for future action. In this context, raising awareness means gathering appropriate information to a high quality. Often the information we need to solve a problem and improve performance is already available to us. We are simply too distracted by other things to focus on it.

John Whitmore says that during a coaching session with a trainee he helped her to focus her attention and raise her awareness so that she was able to "gather appropriate information to a high quality" about her own performance. She did the rest — to a large extent subconsciously.

Because raising awareness is such a critical part of this process, the coach avoided doing anything that would divert attention. He never interrupted. This would have destroyed the focus and reduced awareness. He also discouraged the trainee from "trying harder". Trying too hard is actually counter-productive because it focuses attention on trying to do something instead of being aware of what's happening.

David Whitaker says that when coaching in a business environment he follows precisely the same principles. Raising awareness of reality became not just "What's happening as you swing the golf club?" but, "What are you experiencing in this business situation?"

David Hemery was asked whether there was a risk that in letting people work out their own solutions, you might be seen as abdicating responsibility as a manager.

He said that in this context, responsibility means the decision by the individual to undertake a task and see it through to completion. To generate this responsibility in the other person as a coach, you have to resist several very strong temptations. You must not:

- Lead the other person

- Force your own agenda on them

- Push your own solutions.

One of the major benefits of coaching in this way is that the coach or manager generates the responsibility for improved performance where it belongs — with the person who will do the job. This is delegation, not abdication, and it leaves the manager free to do their own job better.

## Listening Skills

How can we hope to be good coaches if we don't know how to listen? In a coaching context, we need to develop empathic listening skills; that is, skills which enable us to understand not only what the person is saying to us, but also the emotions and difficulties that may underlie what is being said. If we fail to gain an understanding of someone's attitude and beliefs, then we can't begin to identify the barriers to performance and thus we can't help that person to begin the road to improvement.

It is estimated that, in an average working day, people spend 9 per cent of the time writing, 16 per cent of the time reading, 30 per cent of the time speaking, and an astonishing 45 per cent of the time listening to other people. If we think about how much time we were allocated at school and in further education to learning how to write, read, and speak, and compare that to how much time was devoted to learning how to listen, perhaps we can begin to understand why we're so bad at listening to each other.

Ask yourself: "What were you taught about listening?" The answer will typically be nothing. Yet all salespeople know that they're supposed to listen to their customers and identify their needs. Furthermore, sales managers and salespeople in general have a firm belief that they have little time available for all the things they have to do. This perception of the pressure they are under also contributes to poor listening skills. One of the more common complaints that employees have of their managers is that "they don't listen". For some managers, effective communications will have a better chance of happening when they fight off the need for their ego to dominate. Instead of feeling that, as the boss, they have to do all of the talking, they should give listening a chance to succeed.

Teaching listening skills should be a prime requisite of any training event concerned with the personal development of communication skills. We have two ears and one mouth and we should use them in the correct proportion!

*Listening Skills Test*

How good a listener are you? Complete the listening test overleaf and see.

If you could answer "Yes" to ten or more of these questions, then you are doing better than most! If you scored less than ten, you probably realise that you need to practise your listening skills. Poor listening skills are very damaging to both the sales and coaching process. As a coach, poor listening will cause frustration, distrust, defensiveness and clamming up on the part of the person being coached. You will have lost an opportunity to truly diagnose a performance problem or realise an opportunity with the performer.

Barriers to effective listening include:

• Tiredness

• Preoccupation with another problem

• Disagreeing with the speaker

• Disliking the speaker, for whatever reason

• External noise or distractions

• Feeling physically uncomfortable

• Thinking ahead.

| Question | Yes | No |
|---|---|---|
| 1. When you attend a conference, do you aim to sit at the front? | | |
| 2. At meetings, do you take notes and then read them later? | | |
| 3. When you are listening to somebody do you ask questions to clarify your understanding? | | |
| 4. Do you try hard to avoid daydreaming when people are talking to you? | | |
| 5. Do people rarely say to you "You're not listening to me"? | | |
| 6. When you are listening to somebody do you sit so that you can see the facial expressions of the speaker? | | |
| 7. Do you ever reflect back to someone what they have said? | | |
| 8. If someone is saying something you disagree with, do you let him or her finish before interrupting? | | |
| 9. Can you remember all the conversations you had yesterday? | | |
| 10. Do you listen equally to everybody, whether they are attractive or not or whether they have superiority over you or not? | | |
| 11. Can you empathise with other people's points of view even though they can be radically different from yours? | | |
| 12. Do you encourage people when they are speaking to you by nodding, looking at them attentively, and by reviewing with them what they have said to you? | | |
| 13. Can you list at least five barriers to effective listening? | | |
| 14. Do you have a system for remembering names of people when you meet them for the first time? | | |
| 15. Do you need to develop your listening skills? | | |

Empathic listening means that we should listen to what someone is saying with an open mind. We need to suspend judgement, stop comparing the speaker's experience to our own or
drawing comparisons with other members of the team. Quite
often, people who are in a coaching situation feel nervous and
find it difficult to put their feelings into words. The coach must
be able to listen "beyond" the words being used to hear what is
in a person's heart and mind. One of the biggest obstacles a
coach may encounter in interpersonal communications is the
tendency to compare or interpret people's messages on the
basis of the coach's own experience and attitudes. A coach may
advise, question, interpret and evaluate a person's story on the
basis of the coach's own standards of performance or those of
other members of the team. This is unhelpful and ignores the
individuality of the person being coached.

The next time someone is talking to you, observe your own
reactions. Are you giving that person your full attention? When
someone is telling you a story, are you thinking, "Yes, that reminds me of when . . ."? You'll be amazed at how difficult it
really is to listen with an open mind and to give someone your
full concentration. Effective listening needs "will and skill". You
need to *want* to listen and be really interested in what someone
says. Remember, you can't fake it because your body language
will give it away, particularly your eyes, and you need to practise the skill of listening. In an interpersonal communication,
who is working harder: the one who talks or the one who listens? Stephen Covey[4] confirms, "The one who listens does the
most work, not the one who talks." We would also concur with
him that to be heard and understood is the psychological
equivalent of breathing air.

In order to build up a trusting and open relationship in a
coaching situation, not only should you listen, but you should
also *show* you are listening.

---

[4] Stephen R. Covey, *The Seven Habits of Highly Effective People*, Simon
& Schuster,1991.

Develop your listening skills by:

- Concentrating on what is being said

- Ignoring distractions

- Thinking about what is being said, not how you will respond

- Asking questions to make sure you understand fully

- Summarising to show that you have the full picture

- Checking back with the other person that you have captured the essence of their message before giving your views.

Show you are listening by:

- Maintaining eye contact with the speaker

- Taking notes

- Not interrupting, arguing or blaming

- Using reflective statements which indicate awareness and understanding of the other person's feelings without indicating whether you agree or disagree with them

- Using brief assertions such as very short statements (e.g. *I get it*), sounds (e.g. *hmmm*) or gestures (e.g. nod your head) to let the other person know that you are listening.

### The Effect of Not Being Understood

In order to highlight what it feels like not to be listened to or understood, you can try the following short exercise with your sales team.

Prior to an event, don't tell people what the content of the session is to be. Arrange the group into a circle. Pick a subject, any subject for discussion. Allow the first person in the circle to make some comment, in a clockwise order, of no more than one minute about the topic. Then ask the second person to summarise what the first person said. The first person must agree that the second person has accurately captured what they actually said. If the second person has not captured the first person's point, then the first person must repeat the point and the second person must again try to summarise it to the satisfaction of the first person. Once the point has been correctly captured the second person is then free to make their own point. In turn, ask the next person to summarise what their colleague has said. Follow the same rule as in the previous exchange. Continue around the circle. Most will have forgotten what the previous person said, or simply not paid attention in the first place, as they will have focused more on what they were going to say.

After the exercise, ask each person what it felt like not to be understood. Then ask them to reflect on some sales situations where the customer was not listened to, where their needs were not really identified or understood. What can they learn from this? The same lesson applies in a coaching situation, where it is essential for the sales manager as a coach to try to fully understand the performer by asking questions and by effective listening.

In a follow-up listening exercise, divide your group into pairs; instruct each person to ask their colleague questions about themselves and then try to listen effectively to their answers. Then alternate the roles between speakers and listeners. The ensuing discussion should bring out how much better you feel when people ask you questions about yourself, and how good it feels to be listened to by someone who appears interested.

When we look at the POWER model of coaching in greater detail, you'll get another chance to see how probing and listening skills can support the coach in developing a high-impact coaching session. These skills do need significant practice, however, before your interpersonal communications become an "unconscious competence".

*Telling is Not Coaching*

It is less effective to tell someone what to do or how to do it than it is to ask them in a coaching situation what needs to be done or how they feel having done something. In sport, striking a golf ball involves a combination of movements involving your whole body. There are several aspects to it, from addressing the ball, getting your body comfortable, settling your grip through to using your mind to focus on the shot. The performer learns best when the golf coach asks them questions with regard to how they feel holding the club and their body posture, rather than telling them in the first instance that they look awkward. This is comparable to a review of a sales interview.

When the sales coach has observed the salesperson in an interview, it is far more effective to review their performance afterwards by asking them at different stages what went well, how it felt at a particular point and how comfortable they were using their sales aids. Telling instead of asking appropriate questions can result in a lack of understanding of the sales process by the performer and provides less of an insight into what they did that worked and what exactly they need to improve upon.

| Telling | Asking |
| --- | --- |
| External answers | Internal answers |
| Low self-awareness | High self-awareness |
| Information | Understanding |

When the sales coach asks questions of the performer, rather than simply starting the review by telling them how they got on, it leads to the salesperson digging deep within themselves for internal answers. This in turn leads to a higher self-awareness of their own performance and a truer understanding of the ingredients of success.

## Non-verbal Skills

Communication experts estimate that only 7 per cent of our communications are represented by the words we use, while 55 per cent of our communication happens through our non-verbal body language, with the remaining 38 per cent coming from the way we speak and the sounds we make (Figure 11). Effective coaches need to be aware of how they ask questions, emphasising key words. For example, when agreeing an action plan with the performer, the coach might place greater vocal emphasis on the word *when* in a phrase such as "*When* will you start work on your areas requiring improvement?" Similarly, the coach needs to pay close attention to the performer and how they answer the coach's questions. For example, if the performer doesn't sound convincing with regard to actioning their improvement plan following a coaching session, then the coach should probe further with a reflective statement such as, "You don't sound fully committed to the action plan."

*Figure 11*

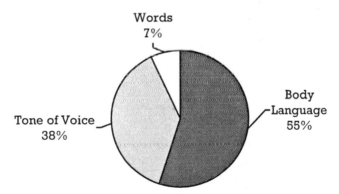

However, it is the non-verbal communication, our body language, which is most important. In our body language we convey our feelings most honestly, so if we're saying something we don't believe, our body language will often contradict our words.

Good coaches get as much response from people by not saying anything than by saying too much. For example, sometimes the use of a pause in a dialogue by the coach should encourage the performer to provide more information, or an encouraging nod of their head will often have the same positive result. Coaches need a strong knowledge and understanding of body language. Aspiring coaches should read as much as they can about the subject, and receive as much training in body language as time and resources can afford.

While body language is beyond the scope of this book, there are two areas in particular which are of great importance to coaches: facial expression and touch.

*Facial Expression*

We learn by seeing. The majority of all information we take in is through visual stimuli. The old saying goes "a picture paints a thousand words". We can't see words, only pictures, which is why it's important to learn how to paint pictures in people's minds. Learning to communicate visually is vital. We do it anyway, whether we are aware of it or not. The problem is that if there's a discrepancy between what we say and what we communicate by our face or body posture, people will always believe the body language, not the words. It is therefore very important for the coach to be tuned in to reading the performer's facial expressions. Do these facial expressions confirm what the performer is saying in response to your probing questions or do they suggest that the performer isn't fully sure? Facial expressions can prove quite insightful.

*Touching*

Touching is something most people never receive any training in, and yet it is an important function of the coach's communication toolkit. It has been shown that tactile people are more likely to be liked than non-tactile people. Having said that, touch is also a matter of culture. In Ireland and the UK, touching can sometimes be seen as a taboo — "This person is invading my personal space!" Yet in places like France, Italy, and Germany, touching between consenting adults is very acceptable, especially in areas like greetings. In Germany, if you failed to shake hands when you meet someone, it could be construed as being stand-offish, and in some circles extremely rude.

If you body-watch, it's fascinating how most people avoid being touched, and yet those that engage in tactile behaviour look far less repressed and more open. It is the last bit — openness — that we want to focus on here.

It's important when building a coaching relationship to establish open behaviour. Openness in terms of what can be said to each other and — just as important for the person being coached — what can be attempted. A coach will often encourage someone to try things they haven't tried before, and therefore potentially may make them look and act foolish. Unless a completely open relationship has been established, then the person being coached will feel reticent about trying something new. Touching is merely one additional part of a total communication system that coaches can employ to help them establish a supportive relationship with the people they are coaching. Touching is therapeutic and supportive. It's comforting and encouraging, and, used correctly, can enhance positive communication. Used properly, it will be unnoticed by the person being touched.

It is vitally important that, at the start of each meeting, the coach shakes hands. It breaks into the personal space, and immediately establishes a close working relationship. Likewise, shake hands when parting, and if possible reinforce the handshake with a light touch on the elbow. Touching the elbow when giving a verbal message adds credibility to the message. When touch is accompanied by a supporting verbal message about the worth of the individual, or an encouraging message about carrying out some practice whilst the coach is away, it will add value to the message.

The two other places to touch are the upper arm at the back, and preferably the back of the shoulder which is simply backslapping, congratulating people for a task well done, or an attempt at something new. Two light taps are sufficient.

## Observation Skills

As in sports coaching, the coach must become a keen observer of the individual's performance in order to be able to provide valuable feedback on how well they have done, or to highlight shortfalls in, for example, their sales interview technique.

Nothing drives home the problems associated with individual perception and the difficulties of acquiring consistent observation more than a recruitment interview panel. It is rare to find two people watching the same person being interviewed who will have the same views, or even see the same performance. Yet good observation skills are a vital component of good coaching. The coach has to be objective in feedback of performance, and as such has to be able to help the person specifically recall any item which requires attention. For a manager new to coaching, this is one of the toughest things to do. The best way to instil this skill is through repetition and practice.

The best way to demonstrate the truth of this is by getting together with a few of your coaching colleagues, undertaking observations of the same events, and comparing notes. By recording a simulated sales interview on video and playing it back, you could all individually present your opinions on what the salesperson in the interview did well and poorly. Do this first without examples and without discussion. Write each of your opinions of the candidate up on a separate piece of flip chart paper and put the charts on the wall. It's guaranteed that there will be discrepancies, many of them major. Then each of you should justify your opinions by quoting examples of behaviour. Your other colleagues should then be allowed to contribute their own findings. Each observation which becomes a point of dispute should eventually be reviewed and resolved by playing the video interview at the appropriate point.

If you have a bank of video interviews, so that this process can be repeated a number of times, so much the better. The main points to derive from this should be the need for:

- Clear criteria against which to judge the candidate;

- Simple but precise note-taking on what exactly was said;

- The importance of analysing how the sales messages were delivered. For example, the use of body language and tone of voice is very important in order to get a full understanding of what has been said;

- No judgements without examples.

Good coaches are caring, supportive, have good listening skills, are as much aware of their own strengths and weaknesses as those of their team. The also have good verbal and non-verbal skills, and are good observers. These are skills that can and should be practised, as they form the basic elements of a coach's communications toolkit. Before looking at a self-check coaching questionnaire, let's look briefly at the need for patience.

## Patience

Coaches need to develop patience. Learning can be a slow and sometimes uncomfortable process and when you have explained something to a performer a number of times, it is essential that you don't lose your temper if they still haven't understood the point or the feedback given. Smile and develop the patience of Job. Explain the point again and help them to understand. Behaviour will not change unless there is buy-in from the performer. Changing behavioural habits can take about 28 days before the new sales behaviour becomes ingrained.

When your sales team fails or falls behind in achieving their goals, advise them that you believe in them, remind them of the endgame, what is in it for them, and encourage them to renew their efforts. Where mistakes are made, try to see them with your team as valuable learning points. In this way, you are role modelling and your team will learn from you the need for patience with their own efforts. Rome wasn't built in a day. Patience in coaching is a virtue, but it's also an essential attribute for the coach.

## How Well Do You Match Up as a Coach?

Have a look at yourself in the coaching mirror by answering the following questionnaire.

### Some Safe Self-analysis

A number of coaching situations follow. After each situation is outlined, a choice of three alternative reactions is suggested. You must rank the alternatives in order, where "1" is your first choice, "2" is your second choice, and "3" is your third choice.

---

*Situation 1 — The person you are coaching has under-performed for some considerable time. You have been unable to spend any time with them due to pressure of work elsewhere, but at last have arranged to allocate a day's coaching with them. This is the start of the session.*

---

Your initial comment:

| Item | Alternatives | Ranking |
|------|-------------|---------|
| 1.1 | "There's a problem here with your perform-ance. I'm here today to help you resolve that, and together I'm sure we will succeed." | |
| 1.2 | "We seem to have a problem here with your performance — what do you think the answer is?" | |
| 1.3 | "I see my job today as helping you to perform better, no matter where the starting point is. What do you expect of me today?" | |

> **Situation 2 — You have asked one of your staff to come to see you. The purpose for you is to arrange a coaching session with them. Their performance has not been good recently.**

Your initial comment:

| Item | Alternatives | Ranking |
|------|--------------|---------|
| 2.1 | "I want you to arrange to show me how you do your job so that I can help you improve your performance. When would be the best time?" | |
| 2.2 | "My intention is to accompany you on the job regularly so that we can improve your overall performance. I'd like to come out with you tomorrow." | |
| 2.3 | "So, why do you think I've asked to see you?" | |

> **Situation 3 — You have identified a situation in which a member of your team is performing badly. The individual concerned comes up with an idea to improve performance.**

Your initial comment:

| Item | Alternatives | Ranking |
|------|--------------|---------|
| 3.1 | "That's a good idea. Do you think there's any down-side to it?" | |
| 3.2 | "It looks all right on the surface, but I think you may have a problem implementing it." | |
| 3.3 | "That's good. Is there anything else you could do?" | |

> **Situation 4 — Following a coaching session, you have agreed a course of action with the performer. You now want to implement it.**

Your initial comment:

| Item | Alternatives | Ranking |
|------|--------------|---------|
| 4.1 | "When do you propose to put this plan into action?" | |
| 4.2 | "What I suggest is that you try this out and come back to me within seven days and tell me how you got on." | |
| 4.3 | "I now need to watch you implement this plan. When are you going to do it?" | |

**Situation 5 — The performer has steadfastly been unable to identify any personal improvement plan. According to them, they are trying as hard as they can.**

Your initial comment:

| Item | Alternatives | Ranking |
|------|-------------|---------|
| 5.1 | "What exactly is it that you want to do?" | |
| 5.2 | "What have you done so far, and what effect has that had?" | |
| 5.3 | "It looks as though you might not be suitable for this job." | |

**Situation 6 — During the initial coaching discussion you know that the performer is looking at the wrong problem.**

Your initial comment:

| Item | Alternatives | Ranking |
|------|-------------|---------|
| 6.1. | "It seems to me that you're looking at the wrong area." | |
| 6.2 | "Do you want my opinion as to what the real problem might be?" | |
| 6.3 | "On a scale of one to ten, what is the likelihood of that course of action working?" | |

**Situation 7 — The performer has tried to implement the agreed plan, but there has been no improvement in performance.**

Your initial comment:

| Item | Alternatives | Ranking |
|------|-------------|---------|
| 7.1 | "What exactly did we agree, what did you do, and what happened?" | |
| 7.2 | "OK, so that didn't work, what else could we do?" | |
| 7.3 | "Perhaps you didn't try hard enough." | |

**Situation 8 — *Just before meeting the performer, you were given some information from someone else who highlighted the performance problem as being caused by a personal situation at home.***

Your initial comment:

| Item | Alternatives | Ranking |
|------|-------------|---------|
| 8.1 | "I seem to sense that perhaps there's something wrong at home." | |
| 8.2 | "Is there something troubling you that you haven't told me about?" | |
| 8.3 | "What's happening for you at the moment?" | |

**Situation 9 — *This is now the sixth time you have met and on each occasion the performer has failed to implement agreed action plans.***

Your initial reaction:

| Item | Alternatives | Ranking |
|------|-------------|---------|
| 9.1 | "For this relationship to work, you have to keep your part of the bargain." | |
| 9.2 | "What has stopped you from doing what you said you would?" | |
| 9.3 | "I've tried my best to help, but it's a hopeless case." | |

**Situation 10 — *The performer seems incapable of implementing what has been discussed. The only alternative seems to be to show them how to do it.***

Your initial comment:

| Item | Alternatives | Ranking |
|------|-------------|---------|
| 10.1 | "Look, I'll show you how to do it." | |
| 10.2 | "Do you want me to show you how to do it?" | |
| 10.3 | "Where do you feel the main difficulty is in implementing this action?" | |

> **Situation 11 —** *When you asked the performer whether they had any more ideas, they said they couldn't think of any.*

Your initial comment:

| Item | Alternatives | Ranking |
|------|-------------|---------|
| 11.1 | "I have some ideas that might help, but it's up to you if you want to hear them." | |
| 11.2 | "So what do we do now?" | |
| 11.3 | "Come on. Try again." | |

> **Situation 12 —** *When you asked the performer to say what they wanted to do, they said, "Anything you want — you're the boss."*

Your initial comment:

| Item | Alternatives | Ranking |
|------|-------------|---------|
| 12.1 | "I want you to start doing your job, that's what I want." | |
| 12.2 | "What do you want?" | |
| 12.3 | "What do you think I want?" | |

> **Situation 13 —** *Your boss asks you why it's taking so long to improve your performer's performance. You have the feeling it will never improve.*

Your initial comment:

| Item | Alternatives | Ranking |
|------|-------------|---------|
| 13.1 | "I have the feeling its never going to get better." | |
| 13.2 | "Its up to him. We just have to be patient." | |
| 13.3 | "He's now had long enough. I'm thinking about asking him to leave. What's your opinion?" | |

> ***Situation 14 — Your performer has tried very hard to implement the plan, but they don't seem to be moving forward. They say "It's impossible, I might as well throw the towel in."***

Your initial comment:

| Item | Alternatives | Ranking |
|------|-------------|---------|
| 14.1 | "What effect will that have on you?" | |
| 14.2 | "That's quitting. I thought you were made of stronger stuff." | |
| 14.3 | "Well, that's up to you." | |

> ***Situation 15 — During a particularly bad coaching session, the performer tells you that the reason they can't perform to standard is that there are very difficult situations at home which they cannot get off their mind.***

Your initial comment:

| Item | Alternatives | Ranking |
|------|-------------|---------|
| 15.1 | "What do you want to do now?" | |
| 15.2 | "We've all got problems. The important thing is not to let it affect your work." | |
| 15.3 | "I think the best thing is for you to go home and sort it out." | |

> ***Situation 16 — The performer is having difficulty implementing any performance improvement. They say, "Look, every time I have a problem you ask me a question. You're the manager, just tell me what to do."***

Your initial comment

| Item | Alternatives | Ranking |
|------|-------------|---------|
| 16.1 | "What do you prefer, me always telling you what to do, or you finding out for yourself?" | |
| 16.2 | "If I keep coming up with the answers, and it keeps not working, where do you think that leaves me?" | |
| 16.3 | "All right, I want you to get moving and do what you're paid to do." | |

> *Situation 17 — When you ask the performer what the goal is, they say, "I have to reach target, don't I?"*

Your initial comment

| Item | Alternatives | Ranking |
|------|--------------|---------|
| 17.1 | "That's up to you, isn't it?" | |
| 17.2 | "Not really. It's what you have to do, but sometimes it might not be your personal goal." | |
| 17.3 | "Is reaching the target your goal?" | |

> *Situation 18 — You ask the performer what help they want. They can't think of any.*

Your initial comment

| Item | Alternatives | Ranking |
|------|--------------|---------|
| 18.1 | "What about me coming out with you?" | |
| 18.2 | "Does that mean you can perform to standard without help?" | |
| 18.3 | "If you want, I can make some suggestions." | |

> *Situation 19 — The performer says all the right things, but you still feel uneasy and their performance never improves.*

Your initial comment

| Item | Alternatives | Ranking |
|------|--------------|---------|
| 19.1 | "I have to say that I feel uncomfortable with your behaviour. You say the right things, yet you don't appear to implement any plans we agree." | |
| 19.2 | "I don't believe you." | |
| 19.3 | "If you are doing all the right things, why is it that your performance never improves?" | |

> *Situation 20 — This is now the last chance. Your boss has given you a deadline to either improve the performer's performance or to get rid of them. During the coaching session, the performer says they will take a particular course of action. They have never in the past kept to any previous commitment.*

Your initial comment

| Item | Alternatives | Ranking |
|------|-------------|---------|
| 20.1 | "Look, this is the last chance. If you don't get it right this time, you're out." | |
| 20.2 | "What has happened in the past when we have agreed this course of action?" | |
| 20.3 | "I'm under pressure from my boss to get rid of you, so it better work this time." | |

## Score Sheet — Put your ranking against the item number.

| Item | Rank | Item | Rank | Item | Rank |
|------|------|------|------|------|------|
| 1.3 | | 1.1 | | 1.2 | |
| 2.1 | | 2.2 | | 2.3 | |
| 3.3 | | 3.1 | | 3.2 | |
| 4.3 | | 4.1 | | 4.2 | |
| 5.1 | | 5.2 | | 5.3 | |
| 6.1 | | 6.2 | | 6.3 | |
| 7.1 | | 7.2 | | 7.3 | |
| 8.3 | | 8.2 | | 8.1 | |
| 9.1 | | 9.2 | | 9.3 | |
| 10.3 | | 10.2 | | 10.1 | |
| 11.1 | | 11.3 | | 11.2 | |
| 12.2 | | 12.3 | | 12.1 | |
| 13.3 | | 13.1 | | 13.2 | |
| 14.1 | | 14.3 | | 14.2 | |
| 15.1 | | 15.3 | | 15.2 | |
| 16.1 | | 16.2 | | 16.3 | |
| 17.3 | | 17.1 | | 17.2 | |

| 18.3 | | 18.2 | | 18.1 | |
| 19.1 | | 19.3 | | 19.2 | |
| 20.2 | | 20.1 | | 20.3 | |
| Total "A" | | Total "B" | | Total "C" | |

## Feedback on Profile

An average profile would be a score of 34 in "A", 37 in "B", and 49 in "C" (see Figure 12).

*Figure 12*

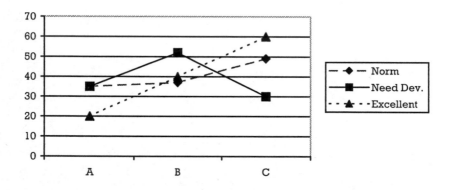

If you have a score of between 31 and 40 in column "A", you have a good grasp of coaching principles and the model.

A score of between 20 and 30 in "A" would show a remarkable theoretical ability. We say theoretical, because as in all things to do with skill acquisition the proof of the pudding is in the application.

If your score in "A" is between the range 41 to 60, then you still have some way to go. You need to consider how much you stick to being in control, and whether you are yet able to empower people — keep with it.

# Chapter 6

# The POWER Model (1):
# Purpose and Parameters

*"The very essence of all power lies in getting the other person to participate"* — *Zig Ziglar*

## The POWER Model

The author Frank Salisbury developed the POWER model of coaching in 1993, soon after attending *The Challenge of Excellence* course run by David Hemery and Susan Kaye. It's a further extension of the model used by Hemery and others called GROW, which stands for Goal, Realism, Opportunity, and Want. David Whitaker said that "GROW is a checklist that helps me stay on track". In the same way that we believe in a structured approach to the sales process, we welcome all models that keep coaches on track and help the salespeople to focus on achieving a result.

The POWER model of coaching evolved from working with sales managers, salespeople and the application of the coaching process. It should be noted that it also has broader application for any business manager.

POWER stands for:

- **P**urpose and Parameters

- **O**bjectives and Options

- **W**hat's happening now?

- **E**mpowerment

- **R**eview.

The POWER model is a tool which can help sales coaches to practise in a very focused way what is often called MBWA — management by walking around. POWER requires the sales manager acting in a coaching capacity to get involved with the sales team. Leave your desk and go into the field where your sales team are plying their trade. Be available to performers, observe, ask questions, listen and discuss performance. Catch people doing things right and also highlight areas where improvements are required. POWER will assist you to get results through your team in a structured fashion over time.

We have worked with many sales managers who think they know how their salespeople operate but confess after a field coaching session that they had never prioritised the observation, analysis and feedback of their sales team before. Comments like "I was really shocked when I spent some time with John and saw how weak his sales skills are" or "I now know why Mary is successful but there were still opportunities for her to cross-sell more" are commonplace. The reality for many sales managers we have worked with is that, because they're busy with so many administrative tasks, sometimes they find they have been concentrating on the wrong activities. Even when sales managers are out with their sales teams in the field, they are often unsure how to maximise their one-to-one time with them. POWER will assist the sales manager to get results throughout the whole team.

The model begins with setting the agenda and reviewing the journey towards excellence thus far. The key to performance coaching is goal setting. Secondly, are the aims and objectives of the performer in line with those of the coach and the organisation? The third stage is about understanding whose actions have brought about the current results — this is where the focus moves strongly into personal responsibility. The fourth stage is about taking that responsibility for making things happen, for making improvements, and for contracting with the coach to work on an improvement plan. The final stage is about analysing the results and making plans for the next stage of improvement.

## POWER

We use the word *power* in a positive sense. We see power as being the life force that exists in most salespeople and something that can be translated into constructive endeavour. We see sales coaching as returning power to individuals. The problem is that we enter the world powerless, and whilst the possibilities open to us are endless, the realisation of those opportunities heavily relies on being given power by others in order to act. In the processes of growing, learning, and being cared for, ruled, controlled or directed, that return of our personal power or empowerment can sometimes fail to emerge. The more civilised the society, the greater the number of rules. We began with Ten Commandments and now we appear to follow a few million laws. It seems that the longer we exist the more we rely on telling other people what to do. It's small wonder that people have lost the ability to think for themselves and, more importantly, act for themselves. We tend to agree with Samuel Smiles,[1] who in 1859 said:

> Whatever is done for men or classes, to a certain extent takes away the stimulus and necessity for doing for themselves; and where men are subjected to over-guidance and over-government, the inevitable tendency is to render them comparatively helpless.

In essence, the more you do for people, the less they are able to do for themselves. The mantle of personal responsibility is a

---

[1] Samuel Smiles, *Self Help*, Penguin, 1986.

difficult one for sales managers to shed; yet to get the best out of people, that's exactly what you have to do.

Using the POWER model as a framework, coaching becomes a series of structured questions in which the performer increasingly takes the initiative in setting and achieving goals. The model is simple to remember, and with practice can be delivered in an easy, conversational style. That ease belies the powerful nature of its potential impact.

### Purpose and Parameters

The first part of the model is concerned with defining the *purpose* of the coaching session and the *parameters* to be agreed upon. That is to say, what is it possible to achieve within the time available? Most people go straight into defining objectives, and from our experience, it is in the lack of clarification of the purpose and parameters of the coaching sessions that many managers and performers can stumble at the first hurdle. Having an unclear purpose for the coaching session even before defining goals is like flying off into the fog and then later deciding on a destination. In any case, the process of questioning the purpose of the session in itself prepares people to psychologically take part in what is to come. As the coach, ask yourself what you want from the session and how reasonable it is. How much time do you have and what exactly are you trying to achieve? Is there something that you are working on for the whole team or is this session part of an overall plan for an individual?

All too often, we have seen business coaches and trainers allow the performer to set the main agenda for the coaching session. We believe it is the coach's responsibility to keep the coaching sessions focused on business issues. That is not to say that the coaching sessions exclude any personal development; however, personal development needs to be addressed within the context of what the organisation is trying to achieve. This is where sales coaching and counselling are a million miles away from each other.

In counselling, the person being counselled sets the agenda and the timescale is as long as someone is prepared to pay for the counsellor's time. In sales coaching, the purpose is about improving performance within a realistic timescale and some financial boundaries. It's pointless coaching an individual who is taking too long to respond. The set parameters should have an eye on the clock and the calendar.

As a sports coach, I may see a dramatic improvement in a runner's time over 100 metres. However, if I gauge that, at the current rate of improvement, it will take three years to reach a qualifying time for the Olympian and they are two years away, then what's the point? The point might be that I make the runner a better person and help them achieve their personal goals, but then that's not what I'm paid for. I'm paid to help the athlete win medals. I have to understand what the organisation wants. If it is satisfied that we perform better than we did at the last Olympics, then well and good. I might be able to accommodate the performer within a team effort. The result may be a better international standing. The point is, I need to establish what the rules are at the outset. I need to either agree with the rules or find another game to play. I need to communicate the rules and my expectations at every opportunity, and certainly as part of each coaching session.

The purpose and parameters part of the POWER model is where you establish and reinforce the mission of the organisation and the vision of you and your team. It should be the starting point for all coaching sessions and all contact with the team. As a coach, ask yourself these questions often:

- Is what I am doing leading me towards my goal and vision?

- Are my goal and vision aligned with those of the organisation?

- Is the performer's goal aligned with the team vision?

- Is the performer's goal aligned with the organisation's vision?

It is pointless working at something that the organisation neither wants nor recognises. There must be a return from your
investment in coaching for the organisation as well as for the
individual. Often we have found that managers in particular are
so busy building internal empires that the corporate goal gets
lost somewhere.

For sales managers, it would sometimes appear that achieving targets is the sole mission statement. This is a very important area for sales managers and requires closer examination.

## Targets

There are two types of targets most often associated with selling and sales coaching:

- Financial targets — results; and

- Activity targets.

So where do they both fit into the system?

### Financial Targets — Results

You may believe that financial targets belong in the rules section of the professional processes (Figure 6). Whilst under-
standable from one perspective, placing financial targets
amongst the rules can cause problems.

If I'm a footballer, I understand the rules of the game and
have to follow them, but nowhere in the rules does it say that
you must win. The purpose is to win, but the rules don't say you
have to win. It is accepted that it's pointless playing without the
intention of winning; however, winning is something that's not
necessarily within my control. If my colleagues and I play well
and to our potential, if we score more goals than the opposition,
or let in fewer goals than the opposition, we'll win. But what if
they play better? What if the referee makes a series of bad decisions that go against us? Winning is a purpose, the objective,
the goal, but it's not a rule. I do understand, however, that there
are consequences in not winning, and I understand that if we

don't win then we won't qualify to play in Europe. We may be demoted. I may be transferred. Even so, winning is not part of the rules.

So how can meeting financial targets in selling be part of the rules? There are benefits and consequences. Some of the benefits are that when I make my sales targets I might qualify for an incentive scheme and feature in favourable sales dispatches in my region. If I don't meet the financial target, I'll lose my job. It's unlikely the sales manager will lose their job, unless they consistently and repeatedly fail. As a salesperson, I don't get too many chances.

The principles that apply to the other professions should apply to the latter. Clearly there have to be benefits and consequences, but consequences aren't the primary focus. To get the best out of an individual, as a coach I have to focus the individual on delivering a professional performance. I can't have the performer worrying about the big picture. That's part of my accountability, even though the consequences of non-achievement will also affect the performer. They know what they have to do and understand the consequence of failure, but in order to deliver their best they have to focus on what they're doing, not on what the long-term goal is.

We're not saying that you hide the desired end result or ignore it. It has to be part of the focus every now and then. You have to check whether people are moving forward and whether there's a likelihood that the end goal will eventually be achieved, but you have to get the performer focused on the job in hand every day, not on the journey's end.

One thing you must do, however, is to make it clear from the outset what the long-term goals are and what the consequences of non-achievement are. These have to be set out very clearly at recruitment stage. You tell people what's expected, the benefits of the job and outline the consequences of non-achievement. You'd be wise also to say how you are going to help them achieve the target and what training and support they'll get. You should encourage them about how many people are successfully achieving the target and how long it took them to do so. And therein lies a problem.

We have come across a significant number of sales forces in which over 70 per cent of the individuals are not achieving target. In these circumstances, it makes it even more critical that targets aren't included in the rules, yet our experience shows that they usually are. The rationale is that because somebody is achieving and even exceeding target then anybody can. There are two issues at work here:

1.  You need to be sure that it is possible for all of your sales team to achieve target, given the variables of market size; population distribution, and competition.

2.  You need to know in some detail what it is that those top performers are doing and how long it took them to achieve target.

From the latter information you formulate the rules of the game and invoke basic training to replicate what it is they do. At recruitment stage, you would explain how top performers are achieving target and therefore what you'll be teaching the new starter and what's expected of them in terms of following the rules of the game.

*Activity Targets*

Given the choice between buying an activity management system and implementing a performance coaching system to bring out the best in salespeople, our unfortunate experience is that many senior management teams will inevitably choose activity management. The reason? It's easy. OK, so you have to push people around a little, and you might have to dismiss a few non-achievers but it's a relatively easy thing to implement and to control. Yet our firm conviction is that it's easy because it doesn't work. It works in the short term, granted, and there's even a place for it during field induction and as a mechanism for performers to appraise themselves, but as a coaching tool, it's a non-starter.

We believe that you teach salespeople about activity, not tell them about it. If you teach by example that activity is important, that's quite different from demanding levels of activity. The danger with the latter is that your salespeople deliver the activity without a corresponding increase in business. We have numerous examples of salespeople forging activity levels simply to keep the manager happy. In the meantime, the cuckolded manager sinks into a quicksand of statistics trying to work out where it went wrong.

Salisbury tells the story of visiting an area sales manager who was having problems with a non-performing salesman:

> When I entered his [the manager's] office there was a mountain of paper on his desk. He proceeded to tell me about Jack Newton, who was under-performing and had been doing so for some while. He told me that he had insisted that Jack increase his customer interviews from eight per week to 20 per week. The manager showed me the charts he had put together showing the pattern of calls and results. When he opened it up it filled the surface of the desk in front of me. It was very impressive. It must have taken him quite some time to put together. Jack was now calling an average of 21 customers per week, but his results hadn't increased. I arranged to meet Jack with his manager present and I asked him to bring his diary. When we met I opened Jack's diary and I pointed to the first name entered on Monday morning. I said, 'Jack, if I ring this person up, will he know who you are?' Jack looked in pain. 'Yes, of course', he said. I said, 'Jack, if I call all of these people, will they all confirm they know you?' Jack paused. 'Yes,' he said. 'Jack. I'm going to ask you one more time, just to save me the trouble of telephoning all of these people, which is what I intend to do. How many of the names in this week of your diary will confirm that they have met you?' Jack paused for longer than he had before. 'Most of them,' he said. 'But not all of them,' I said. 'No,' he

replied. Out of the corner of my eye the manager was sinking into the furnishing of his chair. 'Jack,' I said slowly, 'this is now really the last time I'm going to ask you. When I call these people, how many will confirm that you have been to see them, that you attempted to sell them your service, that they were not a personal friend?'

Over a couple of months, Jack had falsified 80 per cent of his activity. He was responsible, but it wasn't his fault entirely. The manager had forced him to achieve an arbitrary activity target and had abdicated his personal responsibility of spending a few days with Jack showing him that activity mattered but that it isn't the only thing that matters. Seeing more people is too easy a remedy.

There's a distinction between what your role has to be with new starters and with experienced salespeople, and whether they are overachieving or not. The principle is that you train and manage people up to the line, and you coach people after the line (Figure 13). Up to the line is where you set your benchmark — the basic minimum requirement; above the line is where you seek to help people excel at the job. You can't help people to excel at the job until they reach the line.

*Figure 13*

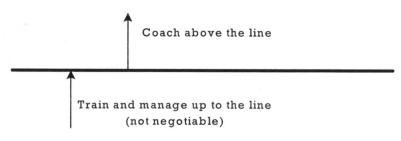

Coach above the line

Train and manage up to the line
(not negotiable)

Below the line are your minimum expectations, the elements that could include the requirement to learn a sales structure, knowledge levels or procedures. Below the line is where you apply the rules (Figure 14). There is no negotiation below the line. You make it clear what is expected and you implement it. These are the rules that are spelled out at recruitment. You make it clear what will happen when someone starts in your team. You do this before they join the company, not after. All too often we've met salespeople on induction training courses whose idea of what the job entailed and reality were miles apart. You must make it absolutely clear what you expect them to do and how you expect them to do it.

*Figure 14*

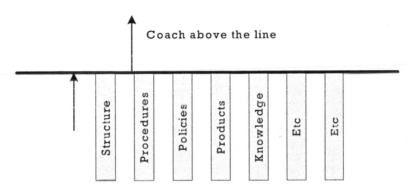

You may produce figures which show that from a particular level of activity a particular financial outcome is being achieved within the sales force or that the relationship between activity and income leads you to believe that the more people you see, the higher the potential results. You may choose to ignore the fact that top salespeople see fewer customers than their lower-performing colleagues. Nevertheless, you need to ask yourself what you want from the salesperson. Is it activity or results? Forget the relationship between activity and performance — do you want activity or results? If it is results, then apply the rationale we have laid out in detail above. If it is activity, then perhaps you've lost the plot. The most important thing to you as a sales manager and a sales coach is results and your job as a coach and a trainer is to improve on performance. Anybody can increase activity, which is but a measure of performance. If performance is low, one of the elements of increasing it can be increased activity. It's the easiest way in which to increase performance by playing the numbers game.

That is not to say that you can't influence activity, but it is not coaching, it is training. Part of the central training programme could and should contain basic training on the activities that go towards making up the prospecting part of the sales job. It is right to expect that people work hard in return for what you pay them, but that's a philosophy that new people will learn from what they see about them. The greatest influence on that will be you and the rest of the sales team. The greatest influence on the rest of your sales team is you.

You influence people about activity by making sure that you reinforce the central training. You do this by meeting the new starter immediately after the training programme. Your job is to check that they have accepted the philosophy of the company (which could include work ethic); that they have acquired whatever level of knowledge was expected (so you test it); and that they have acquired the expected skill level, which means that you test it in role-play. These are three important tests before you allow the salesperson in front of a customer. As a precursor to this, you have to be 100 per cent confident that the central training process works and that the format of the central training programme delivers to you exactly what was agreed. Otherwise, when someone starts with you in the field and they either don't accept the company's philosophy about work ethics or haven't acquired the level of knowledge and skill you expected, then you won't be able to decide whether it's the new starter's fault or the central training department's fault. We suggest you sort all this out long before you start employing salespeople. You and the training department must have complete faith in each other's ability to deliver exactly what has been specified.

The last part of this phase is that you must accompany the new salesperson on a live customer call. It is the only way in which to ensure the transfer of theory from the recruitment stage and of basic training on the central programme to where it really counts, and that is in front of the customer. There isn't a professional coach alive who doesn't sit on the touchline, stand in the wings, sit in the auditorium, or watch the actual performance as part of their coaching responsibilities. There's nothing you can do about the performance except learn. We will cover observations and field visits later in this book.

Part of the purpose and parameters of a coaching session with a new starter should be to check that the new starter has arrived in the field with the knowledge, skills and attitudes you expected. You can't coach new starters until you satisfy yourself that all of the elements contained in basic training have been mastered. If you do try and move ahead in one area while leaving another basic element incomplete (Figure 15), you'll find that the foundation stones of performance aren't strong enough to support the effort needed by both you and the performer to improve. Be careful about coaching an improvement in one area while gaps appear in the basics.

*Figure 15*

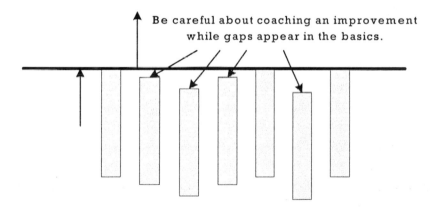

Be careful about coaching an improvement while gaps appear in the basics.

Our recommendation is that you should accompany the new starter in the field for five days after the central training event. You'll come up with all sorts of excuses why this can't happen and these excuses will compromise the successful outcome of both training and coaching. All too often we see examples of sales managers having high hopes of new starters only to be dismissing them a few months down the road. What happens to all the positive expectations sales managers have of new recruits? The highest level of labour turnover in sales forces happens in the first six months of a new salesperson starting. In many cases, we have observed managers extending probationary periods because they were unsure about whether the new person would make it or not. "I'm giving him one last chance to prove that he can make it" is an often-heard comment. What about giving yourself one last opportunity to get it right? If you have made the right decision at recruitment, then there should be no reason why every new starter can't succeed at the job. Think about it. It's probably not a complicated job to do. You'll have done it. Others are doing it. So what is it that happens to so many new starters? The reason is you. Unless you meet people on day one in the field, test that they have acquired the levels of knowledge, skills, and attitudes required, accompany them immediately on a real sales call, and stay with them for their first five days in the field, you will have to rely on luck as to whether new starters make it or not.

It is during these first five days in the field that you teach new starters the activity game. Ideally, you will already have arranged a number of sales appointments for the first week. Otherwise how will you observe a live call? It's no good leaving the new starter to fend for themselves. No matter how confident they are or are supposed to be, remember what it's like starting in a new company. It can be demoralising to realise that the big talk on the central training course was simply that — big talk, no action. How many training courses have you been on where the only thing you're asked when you get back to work is, "How did it go then?", followed quickly by, "Oh well, back to work" with the underlying message that whatever happened on the course isn't the same as real life — and the tragedy is that it's probably a correct assumption. What happens on central training courses has to reflect down to the last detail what happens in the field. There can be no compromise, no negotiation. There's no negotiation on activity up to the line. After salespeople have reached the line, then they can negotiate about activity, but don't be confused between work activities and call activity. What you want are people to have the right work ethic. You want them to work hard. You want them to perform. You know that you can't perform without hard work. Sure, there is a very small percentage of people who seem to be able to perform without a lot of hard work, but they represent less than one per cent of the sales population, and the chances are it is more perception than reality. It is well expressed in the old adage that success is one per cent inspiration and 99 per cent perspiration!

Paul Gascoigne, the English footballer, would appear to many to be a classic example of someone loaded with talent who wasted it by not applying himself and acting the clown instead. Whether the latter is true or not, the former certainly misses the mark by a mile. Delve into his childhood and you'd see someone who was obsessive about football, practising every hour of the day. Delve into his professional career and you would see someone who was on the practice pitch long before his colleagues and remained there long after. David Beckham would be the same — a dedicated professional who practises all day every day to improve his skill. The only time Alex Ferguson, the Manchester United manager, and he would come into conflict is when Beckham, drawn to distractions of the media spotlight, marriage and fatherhood, would relax his fitness regime. That's when you as the professional sales coach intervene and return to basics and renew the contract you have between the performer and yourself. That's when you re-establish the connection between hard work and end result.

The level of activity you want for a new starter begins with what you show them in the first five days of field induction. The central training programme is the foundation; induction happens in the field. If you believe that salespeople should be making ten calls a week, then arrange ten appointments for the first week. Either you do it or integrate it as part of the central training programme. If they are learning to make telephone calls on the central training programme, you could incorporate some reality into it by having them make live calls and appointments for the week they are with you in the field.

In the first five days, you'll learn more about the new starter and they will learn more about you and your company than through any other mechanism we know. You must know within those first five days whether the new starter will make it or not. If after five days you still don't know, then chances are they won't make it and you should let them go. However, you should also conduct a full review of why it happened this way. There's no guarantee that every new starter will succeed, but you substantially reduce the risk by operating the system we have just described. If someone doesn't work out during this period, you must analyse what went wrong and patch up any gaps or failings in the system. Recruitment, training, and field induction are too expensive for you and the company not to take it seriously. We know of many companies where a proper professional approach to the recruitment, selection, foundation training, and field induction of the type we propose here would add five to ten per cent profit to the bottom line.

Whilst you're operating below the line, the way in which you deal with low results, accompanied by low activity, is not to instigate minimum activity levels — we've already covered the dangers of this. That is not to say you ignore it, but to move from a training role to a coaching role, you have to get the salesperson to accept personal responsibility for their activity and for their results. Figure 16 shows how to tackle the first stage. Have the new starter collect and collate their activities for a specific period and have them agree that, whatever that level and quality of activity is, it has an outcome, i.e. it produces a certain level and quality of results. If that level and quality of results is below your benchmark or minimum standard, then you move onto getting the new starter to face the question, "What if we need *this* level and quality of results?" What you want people to take responsibility for is that their actions produce their results, and that these are below what was expected or agreed. Say something like: "At the time we agreed that this is what you would do and achieve; that this is what is expected of you; that this is how we play the game in this company; and that this is the level and quality of support you can expect from me. What we have is a shortfall. It is now your responsibility to alter the outcome by altering the input."

*Figure 16*

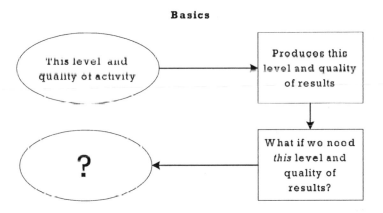

**Basics**

In this way, the new starter has a choice: either they improve the quality of their business or they increase the amount of activity that gets them appointments. In reality, if you have any sense at all, you want the first option, but you'll accept the second option. The choice, however, has to be theirs. You may well refer to the first week in the field. You may cite the level of work you were both involved in during that week, but never fall into the trap of accepting responsibility for coming up with the answers to low performance, otherwise you'll teach the new starter that the responsibility for success and failure lies with you, not them. If you insist on call activity levels, then don't be surprised if they come back to you and say, "I'm now doing more calls but not more business; what do you suggest now?" It's this sort of mistake that causes most sales managers the stress levels we see as normal in the profession. We can't say that professional coaches don't suffer from stress, but it is different to the stress suffered by many sales managers.

Now for the £1 million question — what would you do if you had set call activity levels of ten calls a week, and a top performer consistently only delivers six calls a week? When we have posed this question to groups of sales managers, they split 50 per cent, 40 per cent, and 10 per cent. Fifty per cent say they would leave the over-performer alone, and not discuss the shortfall on activity. In fact, they admit that they spend as little time as possible with the over-performer for fear of upsetting them. In doing so, they miss out on all of the untapped potential of top performers who operate without a coach. Forty per cent usually can't make their minds up, relying on whoever spoke last to agree with. Ten per cent get aggressive about the lack of activity, and complain, strut and posture, but do little other than make sarcastic remarks to the performer, ensuring that they move on to another company at some stage.

The answer? It comes back to what you taught them in the first five days of their field induction. If you taught them the work ethic, then you can still work on helping them to deliver a full day's work for a full day's pay. You shouldn't put it like that, but you live the philosophy of "nobody's so good they can't get better". All top performers in all other professions have the desire to improve, and have the coach work with them. It's only in sales that top performers resist the sales manager's involvement.

When Steve Redgrave, surely the greatest Olympian of modern times, made his acceptance speech for BBC Sports Personality of the Year 2000, he mentioned four people. Three of them were coaches; the last was his colleague Matthew Pinsent. The only problem is that we know of no sales force that has a raft of coaches working with performers at certain stages in their careers. Redgrave changed coaches as he got better. Each coach worked at a particular level of performance, each knew the limitations of their coaching ability to get the best out of Redgrave, and he knew it also. They weren't in competition with each other; they worked together to release the potential that Redgrave had. That is an important point to remember:

don't foster competition internally. Redgrave wasn't in competition with others in the boats he rowed in — he was in competition with other boats. Internal organisational competition is destructive. Have your salespeople compete with the competition, not with each other. You want them to help each other, not try to get one over each other. This can be difficult to achieve in practice and is dependent on the organisational culture to some extent. However, in our experience, once again it is the sales manager who will primarily set the scene and values for the team. The best coaches will help performers to play to their strengths and recognise and help overcome obstacles. They will foster real teamwork. Champion coaches recognise that, as in sport, the biggest challenge sometimes is inside one's own head.

Ideally, your company should have different coaches for different levels of performance, but it takes a level of co-operation not normally seen in most sales forces. Where we have seen different coaches working at different levels in the company, they have usually been coaches from different external training organisations, each with their own agenda, and each not talking to the other.

Figure 17 shows what your aim should be once the performer has hit the benchmark level of performance — the minimum standard. It is basically the same process as in Figure 16, but the emphasis is to move the performer slightly forward. It doesn't have to be by much, but one of the major rules of your coaching regime should be that "We're here to improve, not to stand still". Whatever we do, we get better. The aim is to get the performer to accept personal responsibility for improving, whether they're on target or not. In fact the target becomes irrelevant. You can't improve someone's performance whilst concentrating on the target. The only way to improve performance is to concentrate on making a step forward — by improving how they do something.

*Figure 17*

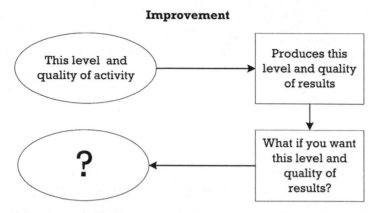

It is important to give the performer emotional strength through your support and your expectation of success (see Figure 18). You need to transfer your positive expectations about the potential of the performer to them — "I know that you can perform to a higher level. I know that you can be even more successful." But be careful about expectations that are set too high, too quick. One step at a time is enough.

*Figure 18*

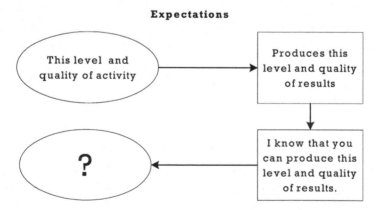

### Questions to Ask

*How much time do we have?*

The response to this question should be followed by the coach establishing what is feasible within the timescale.

For example, you could begin, "Obviously, thirty minutes will only allow us to get a feel of what we're trying to help you achieve, and it's highly likely that we may have to schedule a further time slot soon to take this initial discussion a stage further. Are you comfortable with that?"

If it is a later coaching session, where some work has already been achieved, then both coach and performer will have become used to establishing the parameters relating to time. Be careful if, through familiarity with any or all parts of the process, you become tempted to skips parts of it, assuming that the performer knows the rules of the game. It is always dangerous to assume and the fundamental precept is that ideally each part of the process should be adhered to on each occasion.

Use the term "we" whenever possible. Much of the coaching session is a shared responsibility. The only time that using "we" is inappropriate is at the point where the performer has to do something. "Doing" is the performer's responsibility. Later in the model, when action is being sought, it would be inappropriate for the coach to say, "What are we going to do now?" At that stage, once action has been agreed, it would be a case of, "What are you going to do now?"

*What is the purpose of this session for you?*

The performer must articulate the purpose of the session. That said, if the performer comes up with a purpose which the coach doesn't feel would add value to the performer's performance, the validity of the performer's choice can be questioned. For example, you could ask: "How will this add value to your overall performance?"

Having received a reply to this, however, the coach should then back off. By pushing, the coach may intimidate the performer into saying exactly what the coach wants to hear. Coaching technique can be manipulative in the wrong hands. Manipulation merely results in the coach's aims and objectives being realised, and whilst performers may enjoy short-term benefit, it is rarely sustainable. Classically, the charismatic trainer will elicit commitment during a training event, which eventually is weakened by the passage of time.

*What are you looking for from me?*

The coach needs to establish from the performer what they believe the relationship is to be. We have already said that the relationship is different from that of client and counsellor. Somewhere along the line, the coach may direct, and not necessarily with kid gloves. Coaches have objectives to achieve too.

If what is expected from the coach is thought to be unreasonable, say, within the timescale, then the coach is entitled to say so. All matters of a performance nature come from the performer. The coach may very well be a major influence, but performance comes from within. The coach may motivate, but the performer may remain unmotivated. Some coaches have unrealistically high expectations of their powers of persuasion.

These sessions, whether they are at the beginning of a coaching programme or represent an element in the middle or at the end, are central to the success of coaching. Get this wrong, and it will all go wrong. More time should be spent defining the relationship and establishing goals than in coaching itself.

**Meeting Guidelines**

It's important that your first face-to-face coaching meeting with your sales performer is handled well. Organise it as you would any other business meeting by indicating the purpose and benefit for the performer. For example, you could say, "Let's get together to review how your lending figures for last month have gone. We can focus on any lessons which will help you to achieve your half-year sales figures target."

To help you prepare, you could script your opening sentences. Practise beforehand, as you should for any important meeting. Ensure that the session:

- Is in private

- Isn't interrupted (switch phones to voicemail)

- Has been allocated sufficient time to produce a meaningful meeting. (Don't extend it beyond two hours maximum. Otherwise fatigue will set in and diminishing returns will result.)

You should also ensure that:

- You are well prepared

- The performer is receptive to the meeting

- You have a coaching notepad to record issues discussed

- The performer also has a notepad or coaching log to record issues or action points that arise

- There isn't a third party present, or if there is, that you focus on the performer during the meeting.

## Coaching Time

One of the common criticisms of coaching is that managers often say that they don't have enough time to coach. In our experience, sales managers who successfully coach find it indispensable and argue the opposite — you don't have time *not* to coach. One bank manager we worked with who embraced the coaching process described his situation:

> We needed to appoint a new sales co-ordinator. Now I spend half an hour a week with this individual, looking at issues, discussing job needs and agreeing a structure. It is the individual who must appreciate the importance of

this coaching. I realise that some company managers would say they don't have the time to spend helping staff in this way. But if I can get people to a certain standard, we can divide the workload and make it easier to achieve our objectives.[2]

Coaching doesn't have to be a full day with an individual. It can last five minutes, half an hour, an hour. It can span a week, a month, six months or a year. It will depend on the overall purpose, the coaching relationship, progress made and the coaching agreement itself.

## How Much Time Should You Spend Coaching?

In our experience, performance coaching should represent 60% of the sales manager's available time. This is a challenging figure for some, but coaching can achieve sales results which make the investment in time worthwhile. In our experience the coaching relationship should receive as high a priority as other business activities. It involves discipline on the coach's part to manage time and prioritise the coaching sessions. Consider arranging to meet once a fortnight. Once you agree a time slot, manage your schedule to ensure it happens.

## Coach's Behaviour

In committing to the coaching agreement with performers, the coach needs to commit more than time to ensure success. As a coach, your behaviour must be supportive of the process. For example, if you take issue with your salesperson's late arrival for meetings, ensure that your timekeeping is better. Similarly, if you talk about the need for your team to demonstrate loyalty and dedication to the organisation, ensure that your own behaviour doesn't demonstrate lack of loyalty and dedication. Otherwise your team will have difficulty in differentiating between what is actually important and what you only say is im-

---

[2] "First National: Getting it all Together", *Sunday Business Post*, Excellence Through People supplement, 14 December 1997.

portant. If there is any doubt, your team will place more emphasis on your behaviour than on anything you say to them.

As a coach, you must abide by rules too. Demonstrate genuine commitment to the coaching purpose. In this way, your behaviour will directly and positively influence your sales team's behaviour and commitment to coaching.

# Chapter 7

# The POWER Model (2): Objectives and Options

*"The key to productive goal-setting is in estimating
clearly defined goals, writing them down and then
focusing on them several times a day with words, pictures
and emotions as if we have already achieved them."*
— *Dr Denis Waitley*

Some people advocate that coaching should begin with the
performer setting out their goals and objectives. The coach's
job is then to help the performer achieve those goals and objectives. But what if the goals have little or nothing to do with
what the company is trying to achieve? What if the objectives
fall short of the target? It is an area that you will have to give a
considerable amount of consideration to; however, our stance
is that the performer should be given the opportunity to set his
or her own objectives within the business parameters you have
set. The parameters as outlined in Chapter 6 must be in line
with your sales team's vision and that of your organisation.

Sales coaching is not lifetime coaching — you are not responsible for providing the performer with a ticket to a happy
and fulfilling life. We believe that the coach's involvement in
helping salespeople to achieve their potential will have many

positive benefits. However, we don't believe that it is essential in sales coaching to provide people with a set of skills applicable to ensuring a rich vein of life and interpersonal skills. That said, your own goal here is to attempt to have the performer align their goals and objectives with those of the company. You should, however, also be aware that, at the outset, it is vital that you have set your own goals first. This will and should form part of your vision, which the performer has to be encouraged to share. This is not as difficult as it may seem. Research into the subject of charismatic leadership[1] shows that many followers are ready and willing to buy into the goals of leaders, even subjugating their own previous goals in order to help charismatic leaders achieve their goals. We are not advocating that you have to be particularly charismatic in order to have your sales team buy into your vision, goals, and company objectives, but you do have to work on your own skills and ability to communicate effectively with the team and the individuals in it.

What we already know is that 95 per cent of the population have no goals other than to be happy, healthy, and wealthy. Surprisingly, in our dealing with many salespeople working in teams, we have seen scant existence of any specific goals, timescales, or indeed any plans to achieve goals other than some vague ideas about working hard. Yet goal-setting is an integral part of sales coaching.

An inability to clarify goals and objectives is like having an open lifetime journey ticket and leaving the destination up to the driver, whilst you, the passenger, sit passively in the back seat. People spend considerably more time planning their holidays than they spend planning their lives. Defining objectives is of equal importance, whether for the complete coaching programme, in terms of current work or of long-term goals. Each leads to the next and is reliant upon getting the first step right.

---

[1] R.J. House, *A 1976 Theory of Charismatic Leadership*, Southern Illinois University Press, 1977.

The identification of objectives and options locks into that primal need for achievement, to know that we're progressing toward something and not just aimlessly drifting.

Does the sales coach require any special skills in setting goals? Yes, if you are trying to set goals that motivate. Goals that are either too difficult or too easy can actually demotivate. If a goal is too difficult, a person may either give up right away, realising the goal is unattainable, or become frustrated in a vain attempt to reach an unreachable goal. If a goal is too easy, then a person doesn't feel challenged or stretched, which is what McGregor's Theory X and Y is all about. Building on Theory Y, we know that people actually *want* to achieve more and to improve their performance. The challenge for the sales coach is to set goals that can be achieved given the resources available to the individual.

**"Begin with the End in Mind"**

In Stephen Covey's best-selling book *Seven Habits of Highly Effective People*, he reminds us that physical creation begins as a mental creation — as a thought, a plan, a perception, or a motive. He believes that one of the most powerful habits of successful people is "to begin with the end in mind". In other words, we can't be successful if we don't know where we're going. He comments that every successful action has in fact been created twice, first in the mind, in how we envision our success, and then secondly in the physical production of desired results. Like most good pieces of advice, it's a "BGO" — a blinding glimpse of the obvious. However, common sense isn't always common practice.

Thus, we need to create our results mentally before we can create them physically. Take the example of a forthcoming sales presentation to a new client. If you know what you want to accomplish at the meeting, you can define its purpose. The coaching encounter focuses on the mental creation, the envisioning of a particular result, which precedes the physical creation, i.e. the physical production of desired results.

## Interim and End Goals

Is it a good idea to "begin with the end in mind" at every coaching session? Should we remind ourselves that we're trying to achieve the "four-minute mile" or should we just focus on the immediate tasks of the training regime? Working backward from the end goal can be more motivating because the person being coached can clearly visualise the success. In sports, a coach needs to be able to focus the athlete's attention on the big picture while also motivating them to do the training and preparation. There are milestones along the way and the immediate focus is the short-term or interim goal. The end goal is akin to the well-known analogy about the elephant, which can only be eaten in bite-sized chunks. There will be many meals before the elephant is finally eaten!

The same holds true in business, where the goals are about skills which have a physical and mental dimension. The end goal *defines* the route that must be taken towards the finishing line, but it shouldn't be the focus of each coaching session.

At work, some people concentrate too much on the end result or are obsessed so much with "what-ifs" that they fail to start off right, and subsequently fail to complete a task effectively. All sorts of jobs suffer from the "running before walking" syndrome; it's all part of the "I want it, and I want it now" culture. The coach's role is not to slow down progress but to ensure that progress is maintained towards an end goal. If anything, the coach has their eye on the end goal all the time. That is the coach's job, not the performer's. This becomes the relationship between the performer and the coach. The coach holds the end goal on behalf of the performer, yet it still belongs to the performer. It is like depositing a goal into a performance bank, where the coach is the cashier. Every now and then the coach lets the performer know how much interest has accrued, and how far it is to the end goal. The performer may at any time change the end goal; that is not the coach's choice. The coach merely keeps the performer on track and informed. In the working environment, therefore, the relationship is the same. With the help of the coach, people decide what they want to do and how they intend to achieve it, in steps from the immediate to the long term.

Defining the immediate objective before beginning is vital. Most people have some idea what the long-term or even medium-term goal is. What they have problems with is with the immediate goal.

Each journey begins with the first step. That first step leads to another, and eventually the destination. The beauty of taking things one step at a time, however, is that with each success along the journey, the eventual destination also moves, and goals become more and more ambitious. In any event, the journey for many people is just as rewarding as the destination.

The coach's job is to help define the immediate objective and desired outcome of the coaching session, and then to break that down into its component parts. This may take time, and indeed, if done properly, it should. It should never be taken for granted that the performer understands the objective of the session, and the coach must not be intimidated by the exasperation of the performer as that immediate objective is sought. The important thing at all times is that the coach and performer have to build a trusting relationship which allows each to express themselves freely. If the performer has difficulty in determining the immediate goal, the coach should be able to say:

> The worst thing here would be for me to suggest a goal
> for you. It's a sure-fire recipe for you to feel disappointed
> if you achieve it because it wasn't your goal, and for me to
> feel disappointed if you don't.

Let's look at a musical analogy. When taking trumpet lessons, the author Karl O'Connor went to a music coach in the symphony orchestra. Before playing a note, the coach focused the author on what his end goal was — whether to play the trumpet professionally or as an amateur, and to what standard of performance. Having agreed that the end goal was to play solo as an amateur in a brass band, the coach then helped the performer to identify the immediate objective of the first class. What scales had to be played and to what standard or grade did an agreed piece of music have to be performed? The journey then began. Both parties knew what the end goal was but the focus became each class with accompanying short-term goals.

## How to Set Good Coaching Goals

Goals should be SMART — that is:

- **S**pecific

- **M**easurable

- **A**chievable

- **R**easonable

- **T**ime-related.

Vague goals *cannot* produce optimal results, because they don't specify what optimal means. The following are examples of vague goals:

- Provide excellent customer service

- Increase sales by as much as possible

- Improve relations with Customer X.

These goals can't be acted upon, nor can they be measured. Let's look at revising the goals to make them usable:

- *Vague:* Provide excellent customer service

- *Specific:* Set up a customer help line by the end of the quarter.

- *Vague:* Increase sales by as much as possible

- *Specific:* Increase year-on-year sales by 15 per cent.

To be actionable, a goal must be specific and measurable. What gets measured gets done. In this regard, the sales manager acting as coach should *inspect* what they *expect* from the performer by, for example, accompanying them on field sales trips (see also Chapter 8).

*Making Goals Achievable, Realistic and Time-related*

The goal must be achievable given the business conditions that exist. For example, you cannot reasonably expect your sales team to bring in 20 per cent extra sales during a severe slump in your business sector.

The goal must also be realistic. It should contribute towards the overall company objectives and the objectives of your overall sales effort. Thus while the individual may wish to use the coaching relationship to contribute to his or her personal goals, these can only be considered if they fit with and contribute to the organisation's goals. For example, an individual may wish to make the time available to pursue a personal interest in music or sport, but such goals are not relevant to the company or the department and cannot be considered. The goals should also fit with the individual's job description. You can't, for example, expect someone to suddenly adopt an additional territory or an additional role if it's outside the scope of their existing defined job description. The goal should also be reasonable and attainable given the abilities of the person being coached. You want to set goals that require optimal effort, such that you're stretching the person to achieve something slightly outside their comfort zone but not so far outside that they don't have a chance of succeeding.

While the performer may have a fairly clear picture of the long-term goal, the coach needs to be able to break up that long-term objective into bite-sized pieces which will be addressed in each coaching session. You need to set goals which must be achieved before the next coaching session. Not only do measurable interim goals help sharpen the focus of the whole coaching programme, but they also provide you, the coach, with important opportunities to pat someone on the back and say, "Well done!"

## The Goal-setting Process

Different organisations set goals in different ways. Quite often, the sales manager doesn't have huge room for manoeuvre in terms of annual and interim targets, which often come from the top. However, given that as a coach you'll be setting both performance and behavioural goals, you're likely to have three types of goals:

- Top-down goals and objectives

- Collaborative goals and objectives

- Bottom-up goals and objectives.

As sales are ultimately what make an organisation profitable or unprofitable, sales targets tend to be set at a very high level within the organisation. Other goals simply must be met — for example, compliance with new regulations relating to data protection. It's likely, therefore, that the sales manager as coach must bring certain preset goals to the coaching session. However, *how* these goals should be achieved must obviously be discussed between the coach and team. Even if you have top-down goals, it's important that you discuss the goals and explain why it's important to meet those goals. If you adopt a take-it-or-leave-it approach, you're likely to build up resistance. It's better to have a discussion about the impact of top-down goals and examine the set of tasks which must be undertaken to achieve them.

In one organisation we worked with, this is exactly what happened where the head of sales presented the sales goals as a *fait accompli* and refused to discuss them with his sales managers. This led to hostility and a belief that the goals were unattainable by his sales team. The goals were subsequently not achieved. The following year the head of sales was replaced by someone who involved the sales team more in agreeing stretch goals. There was greater buy-in as a result and higher motivation on the sales team's part to achieve the goals. The sales performance improved following this consultative process.

Collaborative or participative goals are very important to the coaching process. If you constantly impose top-down goals, you'll find it difficult to encourage your team to identify and take ownership of those goals, because they don't see them as their personal goals. As we discussed earlier, when people have an opportunity to set their own goals, they often set targets that are higher than those set by the company. Not only that, but because they identify with those goals, they tend to have a greater chance of achieving them. Where goals relate to behaviour, it's very important that there be a collaborative process in setting those goals. To change behaviour, the performer needs to have a very high level of self-awareness about their current behaviour and have the desire and commitment to change to a more positive behaviour. Remember, it's very difficult to change behaviour: you must first unlearn what you have been doing wrong, and that takes time and effort. Then the new behaviour needs to be practised for so long that it becomes "second nature" — that is, an unconscious competence.

Bottom-up goals, where the performer sets out personal goals and objectives that they want to achieve through the coaching process, can help you as coach to get more buy-in on the performer's part. While any goals must fit in with the organisation's objectives, you may find that the performer suggests developmental goals that you hadn't considered but which contribute to the well-being of the performer and the organisation as a whole.

## Coaching Session

Before looking at good coaching questions to ask performers when agreeing their objectives, it is useful to look at examples of different types of discussion questions you might ask with different levels of performers. (Although these questions are presented together here, in the field visit these questions could be asked one at a time by the coach to stimulate focused dialogue with the performer.)

*For new starters*

- "Having completed your induction training and as part of your field sales work, what do you think we should be working on next?"
- "How will that help to get us on target?"
- "What else could you do?"
- "How will that work?"
- "Where do you think we should be up to by now?"

*For those performing below the acceptable performance line*

- "What do you think we should be working on now?"
- "How will that get you back on track?"
- "How long do you think that will take?"
- "What else could you do?"
- "How will that work?"
- "What help do you need?"
- "What will be the return on the investment?"
- "How will this contribute to the overall aims we have?"

*For those performing above the acceptable performance line*

With an over-the-line performer, your aim is to raise their expectations and to have them committed to improvement. For this reason you need to adopt a far more democratic style in setting the objectives. We already know that, by adopting the "whole-part-whole" approach, any item within the job specification or job profile which is improved will increase performance.

You can use the "performance wheels" (Figure 19) to help both you and the performer focus on what you should work on.

*Figure 19*

**The Performance Wheels**

Positive Outcomes                    Negative Outcomes

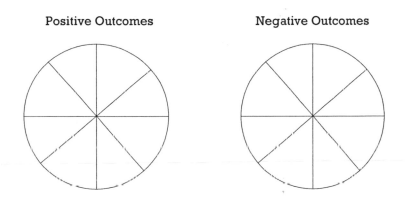

Simply draw two circles on two separate sheets of paper. Using the first — positive outcomes — ask the performer, "What do you do that you believe makes a positive contribution to your performance?" Check out each item by asking, "How does that work?" You need to keep asking this for clarification until such time as you believe you have items that you could help them improve on and you could train other people to use. Quite often, top performers have ideas about their performance based more upon myth that fact. Many simply don't know what it is that contributes to their performance. This type of questioning helps them to focus on practical, skills-oriented elements rather than attitudinal elements, which are difficult to train or coach. Then ask, "What help do you want from me to tackle one of these items?"

With the second sheet — negatives outcomes — simply ask, "What do you do that you believe makes a negative contribution, that detracts from your performance or that you believe you could do better?" Then, "What help do you want from me to tackle one of these items?"

**Coaching Questions to Ask**

*"What are you trying to achieve?"*

It may take some time to establish the real goal. It could even be that the performer has no clear idea of what they're trying to achieve. In work environments, it can be usual for individuals not to have clear personal goals. The organisation may or may not set out its corporate mission, or the sales department may or may not have quality standards or a shared vision. For the coach, sometimes getting the performer to identify the existence of a personal goal can be a frustrating search.

As we have already said, we are very used to being told what, when, where, and how to do things. Faced with the opportunity to determine our own strategy for life, it's hardly surprising that most people don't know where to start, and indeed fail to see why they should.

A good supplementary question might be:

*"Do you see this as a company goal or your goal?"*

Even when the organisation or the sales director or manager sets goals, it's important to achieve organisational goals willingly. The practice of resistance becomes so innate that we also end up resisting our own development sometimes. If the performer feels that the goals are set by someone else, then you should ask:

*"How can you make it your goal?"*

It is important that the individual takes personal ownership of any objective. It's pointless continuing the coaching session if the performer persists in saying that they have no choice in determining the goal. In some cases, the performer may say that their goal is to achieve the company target, which is fine, provided that they accept the fact that they have a choice whether to perform or not. There are obviously benefits in achieving company targets and consequences in not performing to the company standard, but the choice we all have still remains a personal decision.

As their line manager and coach, it is best to focus on motivating your direct report by focusing on the benefits to them of achieving the goal. In this regard, you should match the rewards for accomplishing this goal to their own tangible and intangible needs. By "tangible" we mean rewards of a material nature that are directly linked to their jobs, such as salary and fringe benefits.

Intangible needs are more personal or psychological, such as the need for security, social belonging, esteem, independence and self-realisation. As their coach, the more you know about your direct reports' tangible and intangible needs, the better you will be at motivating them. In order to help them see the benefits of adopting a sales goal, you could ask them to outline the benefits of attaining it. For example: "Michael, if you realise this goal, what are you going to get out of it?"

It is far better for the performer to set a personal objective which is below the target than to blindly accept a given target which they personally believe isn't achievable. It is worth spending some time reinforcing this point if needed. Certainly, if agreement is not reached about the need for personal acceptance of the objective — long-, medium-, or short-term — then you should use a process check which will temporarily end the coaching session in order to give both parties the opportunity to rethink the relationship.

A process check can get the coaching relationship back on track in that it acknowledges that the *process* of communication has gone wrong. Furthermore, the process check describes the problem you're experiencing with the performer — without judging it. There's also joint ownership of the problem and you should talk about "we" rather than "you" to describe it. For example, you could say: "Michael, we're having difficulty in setting a realistic goal. What can we do to get back on track and stay there?"

If a process check doesn't work and the performer clearly gives the indication that they have not personally accepted a goal, it is permissible for the coach to say:

> The lack of acceptance by you of a personal goal makes it impossible for me to help you reach the performance of which you are capable by coaching. It also throws into doubt your commitment to eventually hitting the company standard. You now have a choice of either coming up with a realistic goal of your own that we can work on, or to simply adopt the traditional managerial/subordinate relationship where I tell you what to do, and you either do it or not. Which is it to be?

In some cases, the coach/performer relationship can break down, and traditional managerial relations are resumed. You certainly can't win them all, and in any event, the whole point about coaching is that individuals have to accept personal responsibility, not just for the achievement of objectives, but also for the coach/performer relationship.

Assuming we achieve agreement at this stage, we can then move on.

*"Is this the whole goal, or is it part of something more long term that you want to achieve?"*

The purpose of this question is to help the performer begin to focus on the first step. While it is essential to "begin with the end in mind", you won't achieve that end if that is all you think about. Unless followed up immediately with physical action, mental commitment will always remain a thought and not a reality.

The coach also needs to know whether the performer has a personal long-term goal. Has the performer a purpose? Is this goal merely a dream or are they really determined to achieve their personal long-term goal? Is that goal relevant to the company and your sales department? If not, then it shouldn't be considered within this coaching relationship. The thing to recognise is the continuing importance of the next goal and that there's always something in the distance to go for. In many ways, the long-term goal is never meant to be achieved. People who succeed do so not because they achieve their long-term goals, but because they themselves keep moving the goalposts. When the original long-term goal comes within reach, then another more long-term goal is established. Whatever it is, being on the journey is important. Arriving at the destination can sometimes be a letdown.

The planting of a number of seeds also safeguards against crop failure. Often the people who are the most disappointed in their career are those who failed to reach a single, specific goal. It didn't materialise and without it came failure, despondency, or embitterment. The journey towards goal achievement calls into a lot of different ports on the way. Life is about experience. We are who we are because of our past, and we will be who we want to be by the actions we employ now and in the future.

Sustainable goal achievement is a result of constantly moving the long-term goal. Therefore, as coach, you need to probe the performer's attitude towards goal achievement.

*"Visualise yourself achieving your goal. Now describe what you will feel like when you achieve your goal."*

All motivation is internal. It may have external influences, but the drive comes from within. These prompts focus on the internal drive. They also seek to create a picture of achievement. As we said, success is created twice; once in one's "mind's eye" and then again in reality. The coach should encourage the performer to visualise success and to feel the elation of achievement. For example, in a sport such as golf, a player can visualise putting his ball into the hole as part of his preparation on the golf green. The player should see the ball drop in his mind's eye and feel in advance the sense of satisfaction on holing the putt.

*"Is there anything else that you could do?"*

Is the identified goal really it, or has its identification been more to do with the pressure of the coach? Has the identification of the goal been clearly thought through? Is there something else that should be on the table? It could be that, beneath the surface, another goal — the true goal — lies hidden.

The coach should help the performer investigate as many options as the performer can think of. Some of these, whilst not immediately desirable as an alternative or even realistic for the moment, may provide choices for a later stage in the process.

Goal setting isn't about identifying the one goal. Putting all your faith and energy into just one goal can be dangerous. One of the goals has to be the major goal, the one that consumes most of the performer's early effort, but we all need a fallback position if something goes wrong. That doesn't mean that we have a lack of commitment, or positive attitude. Positive attitude and commitment however, are simply not enough. There are some people who pin all their hopes on achieving one goal and believe that a positive attitude will make things happen, when to an onlooker it is patently clear that they are overreaching themselves.

You may be totally committed to winning the 100 metres gold medal, and have a tremendous positive attitude about the reality of winning it. It may have been your lifetime goal. On the day, what happens if the person next to you runs *their* lifetime best and beats you? We all have to live with ourselves after the event. Having options, planting seeds, and developing new goals all helps. It doesn't make the commitment any less significant; it doesn't reduce the positiveness of attitude. It isn't defeatist; it is coping.

People do, however, have to decide for themselves what the alternatives are. It is common at this juncture for the performer to ask the coach what they think, and perhaps to come up with some alternatives. It is also common for the sales manager or the trainer to then respond. After all, it's quite flattering to be asked for advice. Most people when asked for advice will give it. There's a danger in responding too early, though. Have you ever given some advice to someone only to have them respond, "Oh I tried that, and it didn't work"?

The chances are that if the individual didn't come up with the objective or alternative themselves, the lack of commitment will contribute to failure, thereby reinforcing what a bad idea it was in the first place. Most people fail to reach company targets not because they are unachievable, but because they haven't accepted them. The same is true of options.

The coach can contribute to the generation of options, but only if the parameters have been set first:

> I've got some ideas and some options that you might want to consider, but I stress that they are my ideas. They might not work for you, but if you want to hear them, I can share them with you. The important thing is that I'm not recommending any one. The decision as to their acceptability still rests with you.

*"Which course of action do you favour? What are your reasons for choosing this approach?"*

This is to help the performer decide which is the most favoured course of action and to become aware of why they have chosen this approach. The coach has to be non-judgemental. Whatever the performer decides is right, even if it's wrong. By returning to this whole process time and time again, the performer will work out for themselves what was right and what was wrong, and what worked and what didn't. You may feel that this might take forever, and in the early days it may seem as though it does. However, like the tortoise and the hare, the best route isn't necessarily the fastest.

As with the previous question, the generation of choice is a matter for the performer, not the coach. It's also remarkable to observe, no matter how experienced the coach may be in the completion of the task, how different people find different ways of completing the task, each of them as successful as the other.

We all speak differently, although it may be the same language. We all walk differently, even though we all use our legs and feet. We also all see things differently, even though what we see is clearly the same thing. So why can't we do the job differently? This is the distinction between coaching and training.

Training may be prescription in the early stages. The job in its raw form may have to be done in a particular way, and some jobs that involve dangerous processes must always be done in the same way. Those sorts of jobs, however, leave no scope for coaching, and in any event, performance is measured by a strict compliance to a given set of procedures. The sort of jobs we are looking at should include room for growth, and growth will only be achieved through coaching.

Having trained someone to do the basic job to standard, then growth will only be achieved when the individual is released from the shackles of there only being one way to do the job. Each person must be allowed to express themselves in the work arena in the way in which they feel most comfortable. In the same way that the athlete in the sports arena eventually stands or falls by their own performance, so does the performer at work. The athlete will have learned the basics, been told the rules, and have had basic training, but when push comes to shove, in order to express their own statement beyond that which has been taught, they will need to find their own way. The performer at work is the same. The trainer and the manager will help the individual to learn the basics, explain the procedures, and give them induction training to do the standard job. To excel at work, however, the performer needs to be released to do their own thing. We will explore this phenomenon more in Chapter 9.

*"When do you want to achieve this goal by?"*

It's easy enough to talk about having a goal, but the true measure of commitment to achieve it is determined by setting a deadline. Whilst the coach may be leading the performer to give a commitment, the performer sets the time. The coach needs to be able to make an assessment of the potential work involved in helping the performer achieve their goal, and to establish whether it is realistic or not. Even so, the answer to realism lies with the performer, and hence the importance of the next question.

*"How realistic is that?"*

Here is an opportunity for the performer to think again about the realism of committing to a specific time. From experience, the coach may know how realistic the timescale is, but it's not for them to comment unless asked. The worst thing a coach can say, and this applies to any stage of the process, is: "Well, in my opinion . . .".

These two questions related to time and schedules conclude the goal-setting aspect of the model and represent the cornerstone of coaching principles. The failure to achieve worthwhile goals has little to do with ability, but rather has more to do with a lack of vision and planning. The difficulty most of us face is that simply reading the questions to yourself doesn't seem to work. It's their articulation that adds weight and eventually action. As with most goal setting activity, people rarely write their goals down, specify exactly what they mean by them, or set timescales. We all know the theory. The practice, however, is seldom achieved alone. Herein lies the importance of the coach as a catalyst in the process. The mere fact that an external source asks the questions appears to bring about a positive series of actions. People are at their best when they have someone they feel attached to and who they feel can help them.

> Human beings of all ages are happiest and able to deploy their talents to the best advantage when they are confident that, standing behind them, there are one or more trusted persons who will come to their aid should difficulties arise. The person trusted, also known as an attachment figure, can be considered as providing . . . a secure base from which to operate.[2]

---

[2] John Bowlby, *Attachment and Loss*, Harmondsworth, Penguin, 1973.

Now immersed in the model, it's worth noting that the elements contained therein, whilst initially following a predestined course, can and often do retrace steps when one element proves difficult to establish. It would be quite usual for a question such as "how realistic is that?" to call into doubt the original goal, timescale, or even relationship of coach and performer. Remember, too, that the coach will have goals. Being a coach isn't a vocation, and coaches don't have to sacrifice their own career, aspirations, or even integrity for the greater glory of the performer. At some point, the coach may decide that the goals, action plans, and deadlines are so unrealistic as to warrant a withdrawal. That is not to say that the performer may not eventually achieve their goal either alone or with another coach. Also, within work environments, the physical withdrawal of the coach may not be possible or even allowable. But we use the word "withdrawal" in the emotional rather than the physical sense. We discussed earlier how the coach might tackle their return to a more traditional managerial role, rather than that of the coach. The decision as to which game is played rests with the performer.

In order to help the coach set the ground rules for the coaching sessions, we have drawn on a sporting analogy with regard to the use of yellow cards and red cards.

## Yellow Cards and Red Cards

You may have heard the term "three strikes and you're out" from baseball, or be familiar with the yellow card, then red card, scenario in football. Whatever the analogy, there have to be penalties when coaching someone, especially with regard to the rules surrounding activity between coaching sessions.

Presumably you will set an agreed action plan for the two of you to tackle between the current visit and the next. The coach may have to do something, and the performer most certainly will. The first thing that the coach does on the ensuing visit is to check on what the performer has done. It is important to keep fastidious notes, both about discussions and observations. If you have more than one person to coach it can be difficult, without good notetaking, to recall what happened last time.

The important thing for the coach is to take a view on whether the performer has worked on the action plan between visits. If not, you give the first warning. It is time to show the yellow card, which will alert the performer to the need to mend their ways:

> OK, you say you haven't had time. Whether you have or not is a matter for you, but what we now have is that my time is being wasted. I can't move forward with you unless you practise/implement what has been agreed. What you need to do for next time is "x" [whatever was supposed to have been done]. Let's recap what the benefits were for you in doing this. When I see you next time, I expect this to have been completed.

When you meet with the performer next time, you check whether the task has been performed or not. If not, call it a day by using your red card:

> It was clear last time we met that I didn't enjoy wasting valuable time. You missed an opportunity the last time, you're missing another opportunity this time. I could have helped you as I've helped others. It's time to call it a day on coaching, as you haven't played your part as agreed.

The performer has to understand how the game is played and how the rules work. This leads us on, in the next chapter, to a more in-depth analysis of the performer's game in the W of POWER: what is happening now.

# Chapter 8

# The POWER Model (3):
# What is Happening Now?

*"For when the One Great Scorer*
*comes to write against your name,*
*He marks not that you won or lost —*
*it's how you played the game."*
— Grantland Rice

We have now reached the very heart of the coaching process. We have already looked at the purpose and the parameters that guide the overall coaching relationship and set out the rules and roles for the coach and performer in each of the coaching sessions. We have also looked at what the performer wishes to achieve through the coaching intervention. Now it is time to look at the current situation. This is a vital part of the process. "What is happening now?" is reality. Performers need to face reality, and in essence that is what true coaching is primarily about — coaches put performers in touch with reality. The purpose is to make performers understand that their current behaviour and efforts are producing their current performance. Put simply, what you do determines what you get in return. Clearly, if the performer wants to change their current performance, then they must change their current behaviours. It is all too common for people to blame others and the general situation for a lack of performance. "What is happening now?" is meant to establish the fact that each person is ultimately responsible for themselves. In this chapter we look at a key coaching technique, observation, which we can use to get a realistic, unbiased view of the current performance. With this point in mind, we'd like to focus now on what happens during a field coaching sales visit.

## Field Sales Visits

For line sales managers, the most important area of work they undertake is in time spent with their sales teams. The sales manager's primary area of responsibility lies in conducting coaching visits with salespeople. It is through the continual on-the-job development of front-line salespeople that the company will achieve its objectives. All other things being equal, it is the quality of salespeople that will ensure continued success.

New starters will usually attend some form of training event on joining the company, either delivered centrally or in the branch. Whilst containing some or all of the skill elements necessary for sales success, as highlighted in Chapter 6 there is no substitute for field training and coaching by the line manager. In fact, within 24 hours, line managers can either build upon the work done centrally or jeopardise the frail foundations put in place. For many salespeople, the content of most sales training events represents theory. What the manager says in the field is reality. If the manager reinforces what happens on the course by employing the same processes back at work then training will become a reality. If the manager either debunks the central process or fails to observe the salesperson immediately in the field following training, then the initial training investment will be wasted.

## The Purpose

In client companies with which we have worked, when questioned about the purpose of coaching and observation visits, sales managers have come up with the following:

- To provide appraisal evidence

- To improve performance

- Checking up

- Compliance

- Increased sales

- Motivation

- Training.

When salespeople in these same companies were questioned about the purpose of coaching and observation visits, they came up with a different list:

- Checking up on me

- A free lunch

- Keeping in touch

- I need help

- I need to prove that low performance isn't my fault

- Something for the manager to do

- I have no idea.

Thus, right at the outset there can be differing views.

Coaches should ask themselves this question when determining the purpose of the coaching and observation visit:

> Will the individual be a more effective, better-motivated, and more professional salesperson as a result of the time invested with me?

This statement encompasses a number of elements:

- **Individuals**. Each person has a unique style and delivery. Whilst at the outset we may be prescriptive in the sales process adopted, each person will eventually deliver a performance that is unique to them. Coaching, in contrast to training, recognises the individuality of each performer.

- **More effective**. The primary task of a line manager is to help the salesperson improve results, preferably by coaching. The coaching visit is an opportunity to build a stronger relationship with the performer, who in some instances may have more specialist skills than the line manager.

- **Better motivated**. Some people will say that managers can only provide a motivational environment and that all motivation is self-motivation. This fails to recognise that managers play a vital part not just in maintaining a motivational environment, but sometimes also by leading from the front. People can be motivated by the behaviour of the manager, just as they can be demotivated by managerial behaviour. Managers make a significant difference to the performance of their teams. Time and again it has been proven that manager behaviour begets the behaviour of their direct reports.

- **Professional**. Line management's responsibility is to ensure that a quality service is provided which adheres to internal as well as external policies and procedures. A primary function of the coaching visit is to confirm that salespeople comply with the legislative requirements that may be placed upon the company by the relevant regulator or by internal procedures.

- **Time invested**. Management time doesn't come cheap. Time is money, but like all investments, there is no quick return. Granted, there is a pressure to get people up and running quickly; however, we also know that the best results from salespeople are achieved by way of tenure as well as effort. The longer successful salespeople stay with us, the more they produce. The quality time spent with salespeople developing their individual skills through coaching is the most productive time a manager can spend. No amount of meetings and training sessions can substitute for coaching visits.

**A Framework for Field Visits**

The coaching and observation visit is a four-part process:

1. Preparation

2. Observation

3. Discussion

4. Consolidation.

**Preparation**

Before conducting a coaching visit, managers need to prepare themselves, prepare the salesperson, and prepare for each coaching observation.

*Personal Preparation*

Each manager should keep a log of coaching activity carried out with their salespeople. For example, in determining what a salesperson's training needs are, it seems unlikely that coaches will remember what was discussed on the last coaching visit. What happened and what development and improvements were agreed upon should be recorded

Coaches should be clear about their own objectives. What are you trying to achieve? How long have you got? Is it reasonable to cover the objectives in the time allotted?

If the salesperson is under-performing, are you aware of any personal problems that may be getting in the way? Selling is a stressful occupation and the existence of personal internal pressure is common enough. People who have problems outside of work generally bring their luggage with them when performing the job. If the sales job is all about commitment, motivation and communication, then personal problems can affect performance. How close are you to your team? Do you know them well enough to know when something is going wrong outside of work which may be contributing to what is going wrong at work?

Have you thought about the benefit to the salesperson of your visit? How will you agree it, and how do you intend to express it? Like everybody else, the salesperson constantly asks themselves WIIFM — what's in it for me?

What about arranging a coaching visit where the salesperson is making a sales presentation? Is it something you do on the spur of the moment or is it a regular arrangement? Both have advantages and disadvantages. One of the problems with arranging coaching visits too far in advance is that the salesperson fixes up an ideal day, unless they are trying to make a particular point about poor business conditions. If you have built up a trusting relationship with the salesperson based upon the POWER coaching principles, then there should be no problem in turning up either at short notice or without notice. Remember, your objective is to observe the salesperson in their natural environment. If you arrange the day and specify the number and type of interviews, the chances are that (a) it just won't happen that way and consequently you will be displeased and the salesperson will be under pressure from the word go, or (b) they do what you want, simply to return to the old way of doing things when you have gone.

*Preparing the Salesperson*

Ask the salesperson to consider their own strengths and weaknesses. What do they want to do better, and what do they want to do less of? Help the salesperson to focus on positive behaviours and eradicate negative behaviours.

Do you have a measure of the salesperson's ability? If you don't, how will you know whether they're getting better or worse? It is easy to measure results, but often it's too late to do anything about them. Far better to measure processes that contribute to results. You can do something about processes, you can do very little about results. Results are something that have happened — like a company's balance sheet, they are history. Once sales opportunities have been missed, they stay missed. Unless you get salespeople to adopt positive processes, they will miss similar opportunities when you aren't with them.

Are you aware of the personal interests of the salesperson? What makes them tick, and what is there about the rewards of a successful performance that can help individuals achieve their personal goals? People don't work simply for money, although we recognise that money can be a prime motivator for many salespeople. Salespeople equally also want recognition for a job well done, and a sense of achievement. When top performers were asked what their main motivation was, they said: "Doing what's right for the customer and doing a good job." If they did this, they reasoned, they would reap the rewards. Nobody would argue with that.

Is the salesperson aware of the company's aims and objectives? Too often, staff surveys uncover that people are totally oblivious to the company's aims and objectives. It is not that they aren't interested, it's that nobody keeps them involved. If people are not made aware of the direction of the company, it is likely that they will be going in the opposite direction, or eventually leave to find a company they feel more a part of. People want to be involved. In one company, top salespeople bemoaned the fact that they were selling low-profit products but only received the management information at the end of the sales year, when it was too late. If they had been kept in the communications loop from the start, they could have been selling a better class of product to customers, which was also more profitable from the company's perspective.

## Preparation for Each Observation

What are you going to focus on in the call? The first time you may observe the whole performance, but when it comes to deciding what to improve, you can only tackle one thing at a time. Many managers make the mistake of assuming that because their time is valuable and because they spend so little time with individuals in their team, they attempt to put everything right on one visit. The aim of each visit should be to tackle one thing at a time.

How will this visit contribute to the short-, medium-, and long-term aims of the salesperson? If they can focus on the positive outcomes of the visit as contributing to a larger whole, the chances are they will also have a greater sense of purpose in improving their performance on each and every sale. In quality terms, this is the *"kaizen"* principle of improving one step at a time. The performer is in a virtuous cycle of learning something new, practising it between coaching sessions and then addressing themselves to a higher target. The partnership between the coach and performer is a very important support to maintaining the performer's focus and motivation to stay on the path of continuous improvement.

A good personal aim for the salesperson and for the manager, as well as for the company, is to make the customer a lifetime customer. Ask the salesperson to think about the type of behaviour during an interview that would convince the customer that this is a worthy aim.

### Is it Above or Below the Line?

Are you working with the performer to get them up to the line (the basic, benchmark, or minimum standards)? Or are they operating above the line, in which case you can coach them? If they are below the line, then that is training. You should not try to coach people in one area if there are elements of below-the-line activity that haven't yet been mastered. If you try to coach people above the line whilst other basics remain unsatisfactory, it will undermine the coaching work. If it's training, then there is no negotiation of what to work on. If it's coaching, then the performer has a big influence on what to work on.

### Observation

You should introduce yourself as the manager. The customer will guess who you are anyway. Simply tell them that as part of the quality controls of the company, you regularly go out on calls with the salesperson. Say that you won't take part in the interview, but will sit quietly out of the way. It might seem awkward at first, but everyone concerned will soon forget you are there.

Stay out of sight of the customer if you can, but somewhere you can maintain eye contact with the salesperson. When they need moral support, they should be able to see you. Don't interrupt or interject unless it's absolutely necessary. If the salesperson misses a sales opportunity, provided you have trained them to always ask for the next appointment, you can always coach them to get the sale next time. If you interject and get the business it will destroy the salesperson's confidence. If you interject and fail to get the business, it will destroy yours!

If you can, develop some sort of code between you and the salesperson so that, if they need your help, they can ask for you to rescue them without actually saying it.

During the actual interview, your job is to concentrate on what's going on. You will have clarified your purpose and set out the parameters (the "P" in POWER). Overall, you want to make certain that the rules are being followed. Specifically, you will already have agreed the objective with the salesperson (the "O" in POWER) and you'll be focusing on that. You can't concentrate on more than one thing at a time either. Your task is to focus on what they are saying and doing, and the effect it is having on the customer.

Observe positive behaviours — for example, those behaviours that help the performer reach their objective. Positive behaviour could include:

- Actively seeking the prospect's opinions

- Effective use of point-of-sale (POS) materials

- Persuasive use of word pictures

- Asking good probing questions

- Listening well.

The list could be longer, shorter or totally different — it doesn't matter. For the performer, it represents the positive behaviours for the specific task. It is both motivating and instructive to provide feedback on those aspects of the performance that are producing positive results. You want to encourage the performer to repeat and build on those aspects that they're doing well.

Having focused in the first instance on the positive behaviours, you must then look at the behaviours which lead to negative outcomes. Use the behavioural wheel to assist you in recording negative behaviours. Your list might include:

- Interrupted the customer

- Poor eye contact with customer

- Hesitant delivery during sales presentation

- Poor use of POS material

- Unable to explain relevant product features

- Too much jargon

- Didn't explore customer needs adequately.

**Discussion**

After the sales interview comes the discussion, or at least that's the normal format. When talking with sales managers after a sales interview, salespeople are often waiting for them to say, "Well how do you think that went?" only for them to respond by saying, "Well I think it was all right." The manager says a few words of wisdom, looks at their watch and disappears over the horizon muttering about meetings and the need to be elsewhere. Try and save your full discussion for the end of the day when you carry out your full feedback session. You can't judge a performance on one interview. That's why you have to spend the whole day with a salesperson, and if possible more than one day.

If you are the performer's line manager, it's impossible to be wholly objective or even to be seen to be objective. It's very important, therefore, to ask questions in such a way that there's no sense of blame or rebuke attached. For example, rather than asking, "Why did you do that?", which may make the performer defensive rather than willing to open up, you could ask, "What factors did you consider when deciding what to do?"

Ask questions that seek feelings — not "How do you feel that went?", which always results in "Fine", but rather "What do you feel you did particularly well today?" and "What do you feel you could have done better?" The emphasis has to be on specifics. Get the salesperson to self-evaluate in the first instance before giving your observations.

Make the interaction conversational and keep it light-hearted. It's supposed to be helpful, not interrogative. If you have bad news to give, sugar the pill. Find something positive to say, even if it's only the state of their desk! Whatever you do, however, don't give comments, criticism or praise without giving examples. (For a detailed discussion on Feedback, see also Chapter 10 — Review.)

**Types of Discussion**

*For new starters:*

- "Let's now review what has actually happened since you started."

- "Where are you compared to where we agreed you should be?"

- "What has been the main contributing factor to your performance?"

- "How could you have done better?"

- "What help have you received?"

- "Could we have done more?"

- "What obstacles have there been and how have you over-come them?"

*For those performing below the line:*

- "Tell me what you have been doing, and how you have been doing it."

- "What have been the outcomes of this?" (You may wish to deal with each separately.)

- "So what we're saying is that this activity and the quality of this activity that you have been undertaking has produced this level and quality of results."

- "What do you believe you now have to do in order to reach the benchmark level of output we need?"

*For those performing above the line:*

- "Tell me what you've been doing, and how you have been doing it."

- "What have been the outcomes of this?" (You may wish to deal with each separately.)

- "What have been your major successes?"

- "What barriers have you encountered?"

- "How did you overcome them?"

- "Say you wanted to improve your performance output: what do you think you would have to do to accomplish that?"

Clearly, your job with an over-the-line performer is to raise their expectations. "I know and have confidence in your ability and skill to perform even better than you are." Or, "I just know that you've got another ten per cent in you — the question is, how can I help you achieve that?"

## Consolidation

All the conversation and discussion in the world is no substitute for putting the theory into practice. The worst thing you can do is to say, "OK, what I want you to do is to try that, and come back and tell me how you got on." People can't alter their ways of doing things overnight, and certainly not after a few pearls of wisdom, no matter how right you might be. There's only one way to implement skills improvement: both you and the salesperson must commit yourselves to putting the theory into practice. The best way to do this is to practise sufficiently first until the skill becomes innate and then to observe the salesperson implementing the process in reality as soon as possible. This is empowerment (the "E" in POWER), where the salesperson is empowered to implement a plan of action following the observation.

Get the salesperson to appraise themselves and, using the POWER model, ask on a scale of one to ten what the chances are of them implementing the plan. Then do it, agreeing a realistic review date (the "R" in POWER).

## Traps to Avoid

There are three traps that many sales managers fall into at this point:

1.  Telling people what their performance is

2.  Asking them *why* their performance is at its current level

3.  Delving even deeper to improve understanding.

We have covered the pitfalls of "telling" earlier. It doesn't work and it doesn't produce ownership. You start out with the monkey and you end up with the monkey.

"Why?" also tends to lead to a lot of background explanation and analysis, which is unhelpful because it shifts awareness away from reality. There are plenty of alternatives that are less threatening and more effective at raising awareness. On balance, it's better not to use "why?" at all.

Another easy trap to fall into is delving deeper into the situation because you want to understand it, but it isn't necessary for you as the coach to understand all the details. You are not asking the questions for your own sake. As a coach your aim is to raise their awareness and enable them to focus on appropriate areas so that they can then identify their own problems and find their own solutions.

At the end of this stage it's worth checking whether the original goal is still valid because many people find they wish to modify it in the light of reality.

## A Coaching Visit without Observation

From time to time, you'll meet up with the salesperson, and may conduct a coaching session without observation of the salesperson in front of a customer. This might include basic training (e.g. role-play), setting of short-, medium- and long-term objectives and performance reviews. We do, however, have very strong views about non-observation visits, in that the measure of all of the work that you undertake with a salesperson can only ever be assessed by observing the salesperson interacting with a customer. Although we believe that role play is real in that you use real words and body language, the game has to be played on the pitch to determine whether it is effective or not. What we suggest is that, at the very least, every other meeting with the salesperson should be an observation.

## The Road to Champion Performance

As we said earlier, the objectives and standards salespeople set themselves within a coaching programme are often higher than that which the company or the sales manager demands or expects. Our task now is to see what the current performance is so that we can look at the steps the performer needs to undertake to reach the desired performance.

In addition, it's at this point that we establish the rules with regard to personal responsibility. We need to make it quite clear that the actions, behaviours, and attitudes employed by the performer have an effect. Inputs equal outputs. The salesperson is solely responsible for the results they achieve, good, bad or indifferent. Yet our experience shows that most sales managers focus their attention on bad performance, and in the frustration experienced end up telling people to get their finger out — or see more people, the activity trap described earlier.

In fact, the more time you spend with top performers, the greater the potential return you will achieve. Improving the results of someone producing £50,000 per year by five per cent will provide you with a greater payback than improving the results of someone producing £20,000 by ton per cent.

We begin this process by asking the performer to assess their own performance through a series of questions.

## Setting Up the Discussion

If you are about to hold a first coaching session with someone and your purpose is to help them improve their performance, you should make it clear to them that they need to bring an analysis of their performance to the coaching session with them. You also need to prepare, but the aim of them doing so is to apply some rules to the coaching sessions you intend to undertake. All too often, managers turn up with reams of analysis which the salesperson hasn't seen previously and as a consequence becomes overwhelmed. Insisting that performers come to coaching sessions prepared should be part of the rules of basic training. They provide the tools with which to analyse performance and to set goals for improvement. By making the salesperson turn up with their own data and analysis, you'll be putting the responsibility onto them for their performance as well as teaching them that they should be keeping track personally of their performance.

**Questions to Ask**

*"What have you done about it so far?"*

Has the performer really done anything about progressing towards their goal, other than talk about it? People are talented at setting themselves fantastic goals which, if implemented, would change their lives forever. The landscape is littered with goals that never got off the drawing board because nobody asked the question "What have you done about it so far?" Merely asking the question can be a spur to action. The problem is that, as individuals, we never ask ourselves this question. That's why the role of the coach is important.

We might talk to ourselves, but if the questions we ask ourselves start becoming tricky, we pretend we didn't hear them, or change the question. Even if we ask ourselves, "What have I done about it so far?", we will tend to say, "Actually, quite a bit", or "Well I haven't had a lot of time", or "What was the question?".

Acting as coach, the sales manager helps to examine specific actions — not appraising, just asking. The performer will know how to judge the response. Faced with someone who asks us the right questions, we don't need any judgement, we can do that for ourselves. When the performer says, "I suppose you think . . .", or "You're probably saying . . .", the coach should reply: "At this stage I have no opinion. What *you* think is more important than my opinion. What do you think?"

Moving on:

*"What was the result?"*

By this stage, the performer will have opened the floodgates of self-awareness. Talking about our goals, our attempts at starting the journey and the reality of our experiences is very therapeutic. The focus on reality by the performer, merely verbalising what they internally already know — that the last course of action didn't bring the desired results or failed to deliver all of the results — is enough. We should encourage the performer to use descriptive language, such as "I was ten per cent below my sales conversion target", rather than the general "I was bad at converting prospects into sales".

You are likely to encounter a range of excuses at this stage as the performer seeks to pin the blame on someone or something else. Our inner self is very good at coming up with excuses: "I did my best . . .", "It nearly worked out . . .", "I didn't get the support . . .", "The bottom dropped out of the market . . .".

The list can be as long as individuals are prepared to talk to themselves. Regardless of the depth of the internal conversation, the fact still remains that it is seldom verbalised. Talking out loud to yourself can land you in serious trouble, especially if you adopt the full coaching practice and answer back! We simply don't ask ourselves the right questions. We know what they should be; it just seems that we're unable to vocalise them.

The question facilitates the performer to accept responsibility for the result. There is seldom a need for the coach to say:

*"And who is responsible for that result?"*

The danger of doing so is that the performer can then think of someone else who might in his or her opinion actually be responsible for the failure. It is best for the coach to say nothing. A simple shrug will do. The coach needs to be able to display the correct body language at the appropriate time.

*"What have the obstacles been?"*

Examining the obstacles at this stage has two effects. One is that it could save you some considerable time listening to how much other people, events, and the world at large are to blame, and the second is that the performer will normally have decided that they themselves are the biggest obstacles.

*"How did you set about overcoming them?"*

This reinforces whose responsibility it is to move the process forward. Had the performer taken suitable action before, the session might not be necessary at all. But then, with hindsight, we could all have done it differently.

*"What would you now do differently?"*

Each question builds on the former. Nowhere in any of this does the coach instruct. The coach may have some tremendous ideas and may have seen it all before, but it is what the performer comes up with that's relevant, and it is what the performer identifies as being the solution that will work. There is much greater ownership when the performer sets out what they would do differently.

*"What do you feel about it?"*

Commitment, determination, attitude — these are all internal emotions. If achievement is about emotions, passion, and intensity, then it is essential that the coach put the performer in touch with those feelings.

It is more common to ask, "How do you feel?" It is also usual to answer, "OK", or "All right". We're conditioned to say "OK" or something similar, in the same way that when someone answers, "Well, not so good", the natural reaction is to say to yourself, "I wish I hadn't asked." In any case, "How are you?" and its derivatives has come to be a statement in common usage, a greeting, not a question, in the same way as "OK" has come to be the response, not a fact. "What are you feeling?" *is* a question, and it makes the performer think.

*"Where do you feel it?"*

Now this may sound like a strange inquiry. Nevertheless, it's one of the most powerful questions to ask. Being able to focus internally on the point where either the achievement is felt or from which the failure stems is emphatically cathartic. It brings about "Specific Focus". Putting people in touch with their feelings and pinpointing where those feelings come from is a powerful tool. If an achievement is realised, knowing exactly how that was achieved and where it was felt assists the performer to repeat the process later and can actually accelerate goal achievement. Knowing where the feeling comes from when faced with failure or difficulty allows the performer to focus in on the exact point, deal with it, and put it right. Whether the focus is correct in the coach's opinion is neither here nor there.

For example, in golf, say the coach discerns from observation that the way you as a performer are holding a club is hampering your swing. If further observation highlights that the problem is caused by an uncomfortable feeling in your elbow, then the solution is in focusing on the uncomfortable feeling in your elbow and making it feel comfortable. Eventually, we will most probably get around to dealing with the way in which you are holding the club, but for immediate improvement, whatever the performer identifies is correct.

If the coach is observing a sales presentation that resulted in failure, and in the debrief the performer decides that sitting forward would have improved the performance but the coach feels that not having asked a single open question was to blame, then sitting forward is correct. If the performer felt uncomfortable, then a new sitting position might make them feel better, and in so doing, improve the presentation.

In this chapter we have examined "What is happening now?" with the performer. We commence this process by asking how they would assess their own performance. This helps to raise the levels of self-awareness and a sense of responsibility for their own performance. However, it isn't enough. Coaching is a subjective process, but we can reduce the level of subjective assessment by doing what any sports coach would do: we look at the performer in action. Coaching visits are essential if we want to really know "what is happening now". Our purpose is to focus on the positive and negative behaviours that impact on the performance. In the next chapter, we look at how we can work with the performer to capitalise on those positive habits and to isolate and work on habits that are inhibiting a peak performance. We call the next phase "Empowerment".

# Chapter 9

# The POWER Model (4): Empowerment

*"Champions aren't made in gyms. Champions are made
from something they have deep inside them — a desire,
a dream, a vision. They have to have last-minute stamina,
they have to be a little faster, they have to have the skill
and the will. But the will must be stronger than the skill."*
— *Muhammad Ali*

Empowerment, like many of the fad expressions of the last few
years, has suffered from a bad press. Yet empowerment is
more than simply passing the baton onto someone else. It is
also about creating an environment in which someone wants to
pick up the baton in the first place.

We have spent some time talking about our vision, but what
of the performer's vision? What does he or she want to achieve?
Do they have the will to succeed (as highlighted in the Ali
quote)? Although it should have been dealt with in the section
on Objectives and Options, will the execution of a planned
course of action lead towards the achievement of the individual's goals? Unless there is some connection between vision,
objective, and empowerment, then the chances are that the effort needed to succeed will be less than is required.

In addition, it can happen that on the journey towards a goal, either you or the performer takes a new route. There's nothing wrong with changing course, provided that the journey is always forward. The individual might believe that it is all right to regroup and to take stock before moving forward. You might even hear people say that sometimes you have to take one step back to go two steps forward. This may be true, but who pays the piper whilst he is learning the new tune? In the commercial world it is all too easy for people to believe that resources are easily available to pay for learning. Indeed, many organisations actively promote themselves as a learning organisation without realising the true cost of such a generous offer. Whilst we have nothing against people learning — we believe in the maxim "to stop learning is to stop living" — the question needs to be asked, "Who is paying for this? And what is it adding to the bottom line?" A balance needs to be struck between the organisation's needs and those of the individual.

We have looked at the coaching objectives and checked the performance by asking probing questions to help raise self-awareness and by observing the performer in action. This has enabled us to analyse the performance in terms of positive and negative behaviours. The next stage is to see what can be done to improve those aspects of the performance that are stopping the individual from reaching their goals. We are now at the fourth stage of the POWER coaching model, where we show how the performer needs to take responsibility for making things happen, for making improvements, and for contracting with the coach to work on an Action Plan. We talk a lot about the value of practice in this chapter. The adage "practice makes perfect" is true. The performer must draw up an action plan that will empower them through practice to deliver an enhanced sales performance, to reach that higher goal that is beyond their current performance standard, that is a "champion performance".

## Empowering

Empowerment means placing the responsibility for the performance on the individual. If the coach is also the sales manager, that doesn't mean that the manager abdicates responsibility. The manager remains accountable for overall results and the performance of the team. Managers can't be responsible for individual performance, although many operate on this basis. At the moment of execution of the coaching plan by the individual, it is the performer who is responsible.

For empowerment to work, the manager must have absolute trust in the individual's capacity to succeed. The performer, in turn, must have trust in the manager that mistakes will be tolerated. Too many people operate on the basis of not making mistakes, and yet without mistakes and learning from them, people will never experience success. Empowering people means allowing them to find their way. It is the cornerstone of coaching. It shows an ultimate belief in the ability of the performer to achieve. Empowering people means treating them as adults who are capable of making decisions for themselves, especially the routine decisions that clog up the normal day of a manager.

By creating an empowering environment, work will take on a new meaning for many staff. People want to be involved. If it appears to you that the contrary exists in your company, then it probably has more to do with the way in which people are treated, or have been treated in the past. And just because you tried it once and it didn't work, don't assume that it won't work in the future. Remember, if you have operated in a certain way for a number of years, then it is unreasonable to expect staff to change just because you change the way you treat them for a fortnight.

## Forced Change

The theory of empowering people is all right so far as it goes. We need to understand that we are sometimes taking people outside of their comfort zones, and they will resist this process.

This is especially so in selling, where the improvements you are seeking almost always involve implementation in front of a customer. Everything can be perfect in the training room and on the practice pitch, but as we have already said, the ultimate measure is what happens in front of the customer. Self-development can be an uncomfortable process, especially when we try to change the habits of a lifetime. Experience can be extremely valuable, but it can also act as a major barrier to learning and to trying new things.

Try folding your arms in the opposite way to how you normally do it. How do you feel? It's an uncomfortable feeling. With any forced change, we must go through an uncomfortable learning process. We have identified five stages of this process (see Figure 20):

1.  Denial

2.  Anger

3.  Bargaining

4.  Depression

5.  Acceptance.

It's only when we reach the acceptance stage that we really start to learn and develop as people. If that stage isn't reached, we continue to live in the past and repeat our former habits and behaviours. In a coaching relationship, you aren't seeking to *push* change on the individual. The natural reaction to push energy is resistance. As you can see from Figure 20, when change is forced on a performer, they have to pass through many stages before reaching grudging acceptance. In such circumstances, you won't achieve anything higher than a mediocre performance. You can only unlock the performer's true potential when the energy is coming from within.

*Figure 20*

### The Process of Forced Change

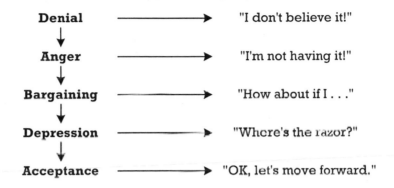

One of the key tasks of a coach is to encourage and support the performer through the setbacks and impediments that will stand in their way. The performer may have to go through pain, self-doubt and enormous effort to reach medium- and long-range goals. If you're dealing with a top performer, you have the additional challenge of encouraging them to reach even higher goals. But peak performers are driven to improve their personal bests, even when they are better than those competing with them.

Sometimes you hear athletes talking about the "perfect race". They feel relaxed, happy and totally focused on winning. They aren't worried about their running technique or race strategy — that has all been worked out a long time ago through the hundreds of practice sessions preparing for the big race. They have reached a level of unconscious competence in their sport: they no longer have to think about *how* to run; their minds are freed up so they can focus on *winning.* In any other physical skill, such as playing an instrument or acting in a play, the performers aren't thinking about the skill needed to put in a good performance. These skills have become unconscious competencies. Their minds are focused on creating a great performance. They're thinking at a higher level.

The acquisition of knowledge and skills is a lifelong commitment. In recent years, the rate of change has become so fast that products are often obsolete within a year, and processes change almost as quickly. If our organisation isn't moving at a quicker pace than the pace of our industry as a whole, then we are effectively going backwards. As managers and as team players, all of us must continue to gain expertise but avoid thinking of ourselves as experts. However, change remains a difficult element to cope with for all performers. Yet by forcing the salesperson to practise new skills, we increase the confidence that comes from mastering a new skill and in the process can reduce the resistance to change so normal in all of us. We need to consciously practise those skills we think we have mastered. Golfers practise, footballers train, musicians rehearse. Learning and practice never end, so regardless of whether you are coaching a peak performer or a performer that is facing certain basic difficulties, the rule is still the same: practise, practise, practise.

The author Frank Salisbury tells a good story about his own experience of change, which we believe explains the process graphically:

> A number of years ago when I was working in the insurance division of a large financial institution, I experienced a classic example of all five stages of forced change. I was the training and development manager of the insurance division, and the building in which my department was located needed to be renovated. Some 600 people in total had to be relocated to other offices, which were situated five miles away. The renovation work would take at least six months.
>
> Although faced with immediate change and not being too keen about the prospect and the disruption, the actual move was quickly resolved for most staff. Here is how they went through the phases of change:

"I can't believe they want us to move out" (denial). "It's a disgrace. How am I supposed to work under these conditions?" (anger). "What about if we left it until I finish this project?" (bargaining). "It's no good, the project will suffer, it's a disaster" (depression). "OK, I can't do anything about it, let's get on with it" (acceptance).

## Check it Out

Your first job following any training intervention is to check out whether someone, in the face of forced change, has moved forward to acceptance or not. It is pointless trying to implement some coaching plan when the performer hasn't rationalised in their own mind that they want to do the thing in the first place. You can't coach people who haven't accepted their need for change. If the performer doesn't know the reason for behavioural change, it is your responsibility to identify the reason or reasons for change and to help them to understand why it's necessary.

And what about you? Our experience tells us that moving from sales management to sales coaching isn't as straightforward as it may seem. For a start, sales coaching involves a lot of doing, and behavioural change. Just because we are managers doesn't mean that we accept the need to change any more readily than salespeople do. Have you ever been through the five stages of forced change? What happened? How did you feel?

When you know the stages, it becomes easier to handle the process. The sooner each of us gets to acceptance the better. That doesn't mean, however, that for most us just accepting the situation works. Most of us have to go through the process. Realising what the process is helps us both to help ourselves and also to recognise what is happening to others.

When we have asked sales managers what they would see to be the main difficulties they would face in introducing a coaching philosophy, they've come up with reasons such as:

- "What about my boss coaching me then?"
- "It's not my responsibility to coach staff."
- "I simply haven't got the time to coach people."
- "I don't think I have the patience for it."
- "I don't get rewarded for coaching, I get rewarded for results."
- "I do it already."

Let's look more closely at each of these answers.

*"What about my boss coaching me then?"*

Just because your boss doesn't coach you doesn't make it acceptable for you not to coach your salespeople. In an ideal world, your boss should be coaching you, but then the world is rarely ideal. Clearly, for you to move forward as an individual performer, you need a coach yourself. If it's not to be the boss then you might have to find someone else. Either you join another organisation which is more enlightened or you pay for some personal coaching. There are numerous examples of people who have paid for a coach from their own pocket in order to improve their performance and move forward in their own careers.

By demonstrating the successes that result over a time period from your coaching of the team, you will hopefully win over your own boss to the power of coaching.

*"It's not my responsibility."*

The implication here is that it is the training department's job or that someone else other than you should be responsible. It's the training department's job to train your staff. It's your job to coach them. What else would you have to do? Sales managers we have discussed this with have included in their role definition activities such as:

- Planning

- Delegating

- Motivating

- Decision making

- Leading.

When we asked them to expand what they meant by planning, they said:

- Preparing budgets

- Analysing manpower requirements

- Forecasting sales

- Time management

- Preparing reports.

Whilst these are all laudable functions, we would ask, "What would be the effect on team performance if you were ill for two months?", or "If you left the company and weren't replaced, what effect would it have on the company's performance?" We all know full well what the answer is.

We assert that the primary function of a sales manager is in interactive interventions with their staff that bring about changes and improvement in performance. Many managers are concerned that in becoming coaches they have to be full-time trainers, and to do this they have to know the job inside out. A lot of managers move from a particular job to eventually managing others in it, and over a period of time can lose touch with the practicality of that occupation, other than a historical appreciation of it. Some managers may not have actually done the job themselves. Whatever the situation, managers don't have to do the job to coach others in it — it helps, but it is not essential — and that's a major learning point.

In the case study material in Chapter 12, you will see examples of coaching sessions where it's plainly evident that the manager is a catalyst, not a demonstrator. So what is it that you do as a manager that would make it very difficult to replace you? In the main, the only reason for having a sales manager in place has to be that they actively contribute towards an increased performance of the individual.

*"I simply haven't got the time."*

Coaching doesn't have to be a full day with an individual; it can last five minutes, or it can last a full week. The determinant of time spent on the process is a matter of negotiation between coach and performer. Those of us in sales management are all great complainers about there being a lack of time available to do all of the things we are supposed to do, but in that, we are no different from anyone else.

Research shows that many top managers actually spend their time in far less structured activities than previously assumed. It has been said that senior executives spend most of their time in short exchanges with all levels of staff, making themselves available for others to bounce ideas off and to ask others questions about their activities. This questioning is not done in a threatening manner, but rather more in a style that shows interest. Yet in most time management training sessions, it is normal to teach managers that other people are time wasters and that you should create barriers and systems stopping them from getting to you. That's why those people slavishly adhering to these systems eventually become totally divorced from reality and effectiveness. It isn't just about being efficient; it's about being effective. You need to do the right things, like coaching, in the first instance.

With all managers, especially first-line managers themselves, it's highly likely, just as it is with the rest of the population, that what one person sees as a lot of available time, another feels is not time enough. It is a fact of life that some people achieve twice as much in half the time. Time is a commodity that we all have equal quantities of, but obviously how each of us uses that time dictates how effective or successful we will be. It depends on how your organisation measures success.

Some companies have spent a considerable amount of money introducing time management systems or sending managers on courses to learn how to use their time more effectively. In some cases, the seniority of the manager determines the quality of the time management system distributed on these courses. Top managers get kid leather systems, middle managers get plain leather systems, and the rest of us get plastic-backed systems — it certainly does a lot for staff–manager relationships! If time is a factor to you, we suggest you read Alan Lakien's *How To Get Control of Your Time and Your Life.*[1] It's full of common sense things to do. In reality it has nothing to do with time, it has to do with desire. Those people who want to, will. Everyone has a totally different perception of time, and no amount of time management training or time management systems will change that. If you value and believe in coaching, you will make the necessary time for it. At the end of the day, you can't really manage time, but you can manage yourself and the activities you undertake.

*"I don't think I have the patience for it."*

One thing for certain is that sales coaching isn't a quick fix, although it is likely to be more effective and more permanent than any other form of sales management. The thing you have to ask yourself is, when did a quick fix ever work. Within a short timescale, the problem is back again, creating more stress. Solving performance issues takes time, perseverance, and practice. Nothing can substitute for practice, and practice will take time. It's something you need to get used to. Ask yourself:

- What specific practice(s) will I need to undertake to prepare for coaching?

---

[1] Alan Lakien, *How to Get Control of Your Time and Your Life*, Gower, 1984.

- What about my patience? What do I do if I'm feeling impatient with the performer?

- How will I demonstrate perseverance over time?

*"I get paid for results, not coaching."*

When we explored this further, what we realised is that many sales managers feel that because they're judged on results, they have to be in control of the mechanism that produce those results (hence the proliferation of activity management systems). Many feel that coaching is something that puts the performer in control and is therefore bad for managers. They like the *idea* of managing people, they like the title "manager", they like the status of management, and yet many don't like the daily grind of managing people. Listen to any group of managers relaxing, and you won't hear anyone who says, "It's great to be a manager." Most will complain about the staff, complain about the boss, and complain about the lack of time, money, and good salespeople around.

Managing people badly is a stressful experience, and most managers manage people badly. How do we know? Ask most employees. Ask your managers how they're managed, and what makes them think they're any different? Being a coach releases managers from the daily grind of managing people. You're still accountable, but it's a far less pressurised environment to work in. As already explained, getting salespeople to accept personal responsibility for their own performance is a very cathartic process for a manager. Most managers are brought up to believe that they're personally responsible for the failure of their staff. Whilst coaching doesn't absolve managers of their own responsibilities and overall accountability for the performance of the salesperson, responsibility is placed both where it belongs and where it's most effective — with the salesperson. Unless each individual accepts personal responsibility, it's impossible to achieve high performance levels.

Salespeople have told us that having a sales coach instead of a sales manager makes them feel and perform better because:

- They feel more involved in the process

- They're released from a controlling mechanism and therefore enjoy the work better

- They're committed to more challenging goals

- They obtain a greater sense of achievement because they come up with the answer to their performance problems themselves

- They understand how their manager can add value to them

- They want and seek help more often from the manager.

If these and other benefits materialise, what effect will they have on the salesperson's performance, and correspondingly what benefits will the manager derive?

We found that sales managers do indeed tend to be rewarded, either for maintaining procedures or for bottom-line results. We aren't against bottom-line results, but the focus of the bottom line will have a tendency to polarise performance between success and failure. In most work teams, the 80/20 principle rules: 80 per cent of successful performance comes from 20 per cent of the work force. Even though most people therefore fail to deliver what companies may determine to be a successful performance, managers always point to the successful 20 per cent as being role models for those not performing. Perhaps you need to appreciate that most of those 20 per cent are successful *in spite of* management. They're the ones who will tend to succeed, no matter what the environment.

In this simple approach, of believing that the 80 per cent under-performing simply have to be like the 20 per cent performing, managers fail to appreciate the significant contribution that is most likely made by the 80 per cent and how under-utilised they are. Remember that the self-fulfilling prophecy can kick in, where the 80 per cent feel undervalued by their sales manager and behave accordingly. Their performance can be radically enhanced through coaching, which has the inherent belief that talent will come out in the right environment and through effective management.

*"I'm doing it already."*

This is a common enough response. We recently dealt with a difficult case of a manager who steadfastly refused training as a coach, saying that he completely understood the coaching philosophy. In reality he was probably the worst coach we have seen, and yet by not taking part in any of the self-awareness training inherent in developing managers as coaches, he was oblivious to his lack of technique. The only saving grace for us was that his team consistently under-performed. As we have already discussed, many managers have a far too high perception of their ability than is actually the case. All we can say is, without a coach yourself, you'll never know how good you are and how great your potential is.

**Empowering Questions**

When you're at the empowerment stage and your salesperson is about to draw up their action plan for future focus, there are many questions that the coach can ask:

*"So what do you have to do about it now?"*

At this point, the performer could say, "I suppose what you're telling me is . . ." or something similar. Many performers have a lifetime of being told what to do behind them, and even at this stage in the process may seek to put the responsibility for potential failure onto the coach. The coach needs to make the performer absolutely aware of whose responsibility it now is to move forward. For example: "I'm not telling you anything at this stage. Whatever you do is up to you. You are responsible for your performance."

*"What is it you want to do now?"*

Having gained that commitment, it is important to reinforce it: "Is that what you want to do? How much trust do you have in your ability to do it?"

At this juncture, it becomes important to measure the level of commitment the performer has. Is the performer doing it because they really want to, or is it some external influence, such as the coach, that is making them do it? Unless the performer is convinced both that they have the ability and that success is possible, it is likely that they will fail. A strong supplementary question now is:

*"On a scale of one to ten, what is the likelihood of you succeeding or of carrying out this task?"*

If the performer identifies the likelihood of success as being at seven or below, then the chances are that they won't succeed, and the process should begin again. The coach may also decide that further investment of their time is now questionable. Remember, coaching is not counselling. The coach has aims, and in the case of the coach being a manager, they may also have urgent organisational goals to achieve. It is quite in order for the coach, having heard a commitment of less than seven, to say, "I now have a problem in investing more of my time in something which you feel has a less than certain chance of success."

The discussion following this statement can be enlightening. At this stage, the coach and performer can revisit the goal, redefine the deadline, or examine why the performer doesn't appear totally committed. It could be the wrong goal, which is why the questions are powerful. Many people invest energy in ill-defined goals, which, because they haven't been examined in detail, often fail to be realised.

*"What immediate support do you need?"*

The contract is a joint one. The performer needs to feel that there is support, and the coach needs to offer it. The achievement of the goal may also require additional resources, such as equipment, people support or further training. This is that last chance to get it right before going for the goal.

*"Can you see any personal barriers that might hold you back?"*

It is useful at this stage to help the performer to consider the types of personal issues that might cause them to be deflected from their goal. You may find that the person in certain situations lacks confidence. Through visualising the performance of the goal and talking through the issues which can upset the person's concentration or focus, the performer can address the problems in advance in an environment where they feel safe.

*"Are there any other issues that could impede your performance?"*

There may be certain market or organisational changes which the performer feels will reduce his or her chance of success. It is important to anticipate and deal with these issues before the coaching session ends, as these external barriers to performance could become the excuses for non-completion. In answering this question, the performer is obliged to think of contingency plans in advance.

*"Do it!"*

The coach empowers the individual to achieve the goal. The instruction is directive. Throughout the whole process, the coach has avoided telling the performer what to do, precisely because the time to tell is now and it therefore has maximum impact. That is not to say that during the rest of the process the coach may not offer advice, but only after asking for permission.

"Do it" should be the first and only time in the initial stages that the coach tells the performer what to do, and yet the coach isn't really telling the performer *what* to do, but rather merely telling the performer to do what the performer has identified as the correct course of action. In this phase, we should be discussing specifically the performer's commitment to practise a new skill, checking with the performer when they will start, the frequency with which they will be able to practise the skill and so on. Get the performer to discuss specific dates, clients, etc.

When setting out their action plan, it's vital that the salesperson doesn't bite off more than they can chew. In other words, the action plan should have a maximum of three points for improvement. An improvement in performance typically stems from a focus on one step at a time — remember, we're trying to lift the bar just one little notch at a time.

In summary, once the performer has set challenging but attainable goals, the hard work of reaching those goals begins. Empowering is about drawing up the action plan to achieve your objectives. In this plan, you need to address the practical issues of when, where and how you will practise your new learning, the personal barriers that might hold you back and the supports you may need to achieve your objectives. The performer may need additional training, new equipment or on-the-job advice and support. It's important in this phase that the performer understands and buys into the fact that they're responsible for achieving their objectives. In questioning the performer, the coach needs to ensure that the performer is committed to achieving their objectives. If there is any doubt, then the objectives themselves need to be re-examined.

# Chapter 10

# The POWER Model (5): Review

*"The greatest accomplishment is not in never failing, but in rising again after you fall."* — Vince Lombardi

One of the most challenging aspects of achieving peak performance is the requirement to change deeply embedded habits. Training or pep talks on their own can't help you to change behaviour. The review of a performance is a very powerful tool to help embed behavioural change. You can review immediately after a course of action has been agreed: you can ask the performer to role-play a particular interaction that requires improvement. You can also review a performance after the salesperson has been given a period of time to practise a new task. The review uses the coaching tools of questioning, observation, role-play and feedback. In this chapter, we will examine what the R means in our POWER model. Specifically, we will focus on how you as coach can keep the performer on track, even if they go slightly off course every now and then!

A review is used at two stages in the coaching process: immediately after a new course of action has been followed and at the commencement of a session within a whole coaching programme.

## Immediate Review

Coaching only works if, following agreement on a course of action, the coach then observes the performer carrying out the task immediately. The sooner the review takes place after observation, the more powerful the impact on the performer. One of the biggest problems with the manager as a coach is that managers are prone to agreeing courses of action and then abdicating responsibility by saying, "Come back and see me next week and tell me how you got on."

Salespeople who know how to play this game come back later and say, "I did what you said, and it didn't work!"

This process may be the first time that a performer has truly committed themselves to a specific course of action. Strange to say, many people fail because they're frightened of not succeeding, and therefore rarely put themselves in the position of a risk of failure. What they don't understand is that the points of failure and success cross at the same junction. Succeeding or failing shouldn't be the primary focus in the first instance. All that each individual can do is to focus on their own performance, and commit themselves to action.

By immediately offering to observe, the coach again tests the commitment of the performer. This also shows the commitment of the coach to help the performer succeed.

## Progress Review

A coaching partnership takes place over time, and that is its special value. We review performance over time and raise the performance bar a little at each session, but we also observe what has happened and check back on our agreed action plan from the previous coaching session.

Did the performer do what they said they would do? This discussion can't take place without the coach having been there to observe what happened. Getting feedback from a performer about what they did and what happened without first-hand knowledge is a pointless and fruitless exchange. The coach observes and compares against what was agreed:

"What were you trying to do? What did you do? What did you feel? Where did you feel it? What would you do differently?"

The process is the same as that which went before. The added advantage is that now both coach and performer have additional data to hand — experience of the event. It can prove invaluable.

## A Champion's Journal

If it isn't written down, it didn't happen. Unless you write something down at the time and refer to it in the future, you and the performer will have to rely on memory. It is virtually a certainty that your recollection of events will be different from that of the performer's. The Champion's Journal (see Chapter 11) is the ideal way to record plans and achievements and can be used to track performance over a series of coaching sessions. It is vital that as a coach you keep a log to record and monitor the action plan. In turn, the performer must also keep a copy of their agreed action plan.

On the other hand, a Champion's Journal is a personal log for training and development that the performer undertakes to keep for the duration of the coaching programme. This diary allows the performer to record activities or achievements that they are proud of or that are important milestones to reaching a personal goal or ambition.

While the performer ultimately chooses to use the diary or not, it's worth remembering that they will find it hard to stay on track if they aren't aiming towards goals that are clearly stated.

Equally, if they don't log their successes, the development needs they have, and the positive changes that will result, how can they be certain they have actually achieved them? Sometimes it can be comforting to us all to be able to remind ourselves of our ability to achieve and our willingness to learn through looking back at the written word. This exercise can also be motivational for the performer to continue on the onward path of achievement.

## Changing Behaviour

While the performer may have understood and agreed to improve specific skills or behaviour, they're likely to have found the reality of trying to change behaviour on the job much more difficult than they thought. In the review session you may need to discuss the special challenges of changing behaviour. You may also encounter some resistance from performers who think you're trying to change their personality!

Many people confuse personality with behaviour, so it's important to emphasise that you are not trying to change the performer's personality. A person's personality is unique and includes characteristics such as temperament, emotional and mental traits and *patterns* of behaviour. In a coaching relationship, we're concerned only with the performer's observable behaviour on the job, and that behaviour can be changed, but it takes a lot of time and effort.

You may find that the performer doesn't accept that behavioural change is possible, but you can illustrate how much the performer has changed by asking questions about how they approached the job when they first started working compared to their current approach. While we learn a lot about how to interact with people from a very early age, we also learn much of our behaviour on the job. Depending on the type of organisation, the leadership style and the people who we learn from at work, we can grow or improve — or regress and worsen. We are changing and adapting all the time. The idea that we're stuck in some sort of behavioural groove just doesn't stack up.

Remembering that selling is a physical skill like sports or the performing arts. Behavioural change in all these activities comes about through experimentation and practice. The performer will also typically find that they reduce performance while they're experimenting and practising. It may take weeks or even months. We need to practise a new behaviour until it becomes an unconscious competence (see Chapter 1).

**Role-Plays**

We've discussed the importance of practice a good deal. It's not unusual, however, for salespeople to find the notion of practising before they go out in front of a "live audience" (their customers) fussy, unnecessary and even insulting to their intelligence. Our own research has shown that salespeople will always choose training on product knowledge when asked to identify training needs, while role play consistently is at the bottom of the list. Most salespeople, except the good ones, will try to avoid any environment in which they have to sell or practise their selling skills.

The letters ROLE could well stand for "Rehearsal of Life Events", because role-play sessions are meant to prepare people for situations that might happen. The role-plays you use should be about situations that have happened or are likely to happen in the future. To prepare for this, you should build up a series of case studies based on the combined experience of the sales force. Take time to develop some scripts and scenarios that will produce the ideal learning point you are seeking to achieve.

When faced with a performer who is reluctant to participate in role-plays, ask them: "If you don't believe in the need to practise through role-play, then are you saying that you'll practise live in a customer interview?" The penny should drop! Professionals in sport or the performing arts must practise before performing live. Poor performance through lack of rehearsal time equals poor sales.

*Be Positive*

When reviewing team or individual performances, the sales coach should remember the lessons highlighted earlier in the Pygmalion effect. In a coaching role, it is imperative that you affirm individuals' efforts to enhance their own performance. The process starts with the coach in that how you feel about yourself will impact on how others see or feel about you. If you feel optimistic and believe that your sales team can deliver the required results, then your positive style will affect your people and their self-belief. The reverse is also true. In case you think that your mood or outlook is outside your own control, remember that you, and you alone, have the power to choose your own outlook and response in any situation. Victor Frankl put it succinctly:

> The last of the human freedoms (is) to choose one's atti-
> tude in any given set of circumstances, to choose one's
> own way.[1]

No sales team, nor indeed any team, will perform to its true potential unless people in the team feel valued. The coach is key, as you can provide the necessary support structure for increased individual productivity. This means, for example, that the sales manager should always be on the lookout for positive behaviours or results. Never allow a sales interview in which you have observed the performer in action go by without finding something positive to say — even where a sale didn't result. For example, you could say, "Well done, Mike, for getting the client to agree to you following up in six months' time to review his financial circumstances."

The coach's attitude and the language used are very important when giving feedback. When you have positive things to say to the performer, use words like *great, excellent, top class, or terrific* when commenting on their fine performance. Don't wait for a big sale to offer praise. Instead, recognise the small steps of achievement and in this way plant the seeds of success for a bigger harvest. Your team will respond more positively to your expressions of enthusiasm and optimism. This becomes a reinforcer and they're much more likely to repeat their successful sales behaviours. In this way, it can become a cycle of success. Over time, watch the body language of your sales team change for the better:

---

[1] Victor Frankl, *Man's Search for Meaning*, First Washington Square Press, 1985.

Their expressions, postures and attitudes change when you enter the room. Their backs will straighten, the corners of their mouths will turn up, and they will unconsciously reflect your positive spirit, in spite of themselves. But here's the good news: managers who have tested upbeat language in the workplace report that after a while just entering the office or building will produce positive staff response.[2]

However, offer praise only when it's warranted. Over-praising when there isn't any evidence of achievement or effort won't fool anyone. Indeed, it can do more harm than good in that it will tend to negate genuinely positive output.

## Be Honest

When coaching Wexford, the All Ireland Hurling champions of 1996, to success, coach Liam Griffin stated that their success was built on the principles of trust and honesty.[3] We will look at the need for trust shortly. This need for honesty between coach and players is a common feature among other successful sports teams and in the performing arts, and it holds true for the business coach. When reviewing someone's performance after their own self-analysis, be direct, open and honest with them. Focus on what you actually observed. Highlight with the performer where you have points of agreement with their own analysis but also don't be afraid to highlight areas where you disagree. Cite specific examples in your discussion. You owe it to them and to yourself to be honest. Tell them the truth, even when at times it will hurt. If you take the easy way out and fudge feedback in a review with your performers, it will come back to haunt you. How can people progress unless they know how they are currently performing?

------

[2] William Hendricks (ed.), *Coaching, Mentoring and Managing*, Career Press, 1996.

[3] *Coaching Champions: The Wexford Team Story*, a training video made by First Active plc Training & Development, 1996.

**Feedback**

Feedback is sometimes called the "breakfast of champions". Providing feedback is an essential part of coaching. There are two main reasons for giving feedback: to reward people when they're doing well, known as motivational feedback; and to help and encourage performers to improve, termed developmental feedback. How much, how often and how you do it is critical. Too much, too often and too critical can result in a demotivated performer who only learns how to comply, not to excel. Your job as a coach is to give feedback in such a way that the performer is encouraged to move on. That doesn't mean ignoring areas that require improvement, but you have to understand that none of us likes negative feedback.

*Focus on Behaviour, Not Attitude*

Never mention attitude (e.g. "You don't seem to have the right attitude for the job"). Attitude is a consequence of behaviour. You could be right that their attitude is wrong, yet you'll never change it by talking about it. In the same way that talking about a failure to meet targets won't result in target achievement, talking about a bad attitude won't result in achieving positive behaviour.

Failure to achieve target is a consequence of actions taken by the salesperson. The way you improve achievement of target is to examine the actions taken by the salesperson. The way to improve attitude is to examine the behaviours that cause the attitude. You can retrain behaviours, but you can't retrain attitude. Behaviours can be observed; attitudes can only be felt.

*How to Deliver High-Impact Feedback*

Throughout the whole coaching relationship, you are providing feedback or acting as a mirror to the performer so that they can "see" themselves more clearly. Feedback is essential to employee development. For feedback to be effective, it must be given in a safe, collaborative climate that is non-threatening. If you adopt a cross-examining style, the performer will become defensive.

The following tips can be applied in many coaching and non-coaching situations:

1. **Time and place**. Feedback should take place as quickly as possible after the event in order to achieve maximum impact. Always conduct feedback sessions in private and ensure that there are no interruptions, such as phone calls. If either the coach or performer is under stress, postpone the feedback session.

2. **Encourage the performer to do the talking**. Use a questioning approach so that you give the performer the opportunity to discover their own learning as well as letting them know that you value their opinion.

3. **Establish trust**. The need for trust can often be overlooked and yet it is an essential element in coaching for both sports and the performing arts. It's also essential in business. Your sales team should believe that you'll support them in their performance efforts and that your role is to help them to deliver on the sales goals. In the feedback session, adopt a partnership relationship. If you can show that you're on the same side as the performer, i.e. there to help and support, not admonish and undermine, then you'll help to build up trust and achieve better results. Where a performance problem exists, for example, don't say, "You've got a problem", instead say, "We've got a problem." This will help the performer to open up in the review more because you have adopted a joint "we're in this together" approach. The responsibility for performance still rests with the performer.

4. **Diagnose before you prescribe**. Try to really understand the performer's barriers and motivations. Listen closely to what they say and how they say it, then make sure they feel understood and accepted. You don't have to approve, and

often you won't. You just need to demonstrate that you understand.

5. **Don't hog the controls**. As the line manager, you will probably be perceived as having all the power. Share the control by allowing the performer to shape some of the feedback process, e.g. the focus of the feedback session. Remember that the performer's perception of what's important is more significant than your own observations.

6. **Treat feedback as information, not as a value judgment**. Present feedback in neutral terms rather than labelling the behaviour or the person. Reward achievement by catching the performer doing things right.

7. **Relate to performance objectives and expectations and keep the focus on behaviour, not personality or attitude**. For example: "I felt that you didn't give your full attention to the sales enquiry" is far more beneficial than a sweeping statement such as, "You're careless when dealing with sales enquiries."

8. **Guide the feedback session towards action points, a deadline and a commitment to review**.

9. **Concentrate on a maximum of three action points**. Reach agreement on benefits and consequences of the salesperson delivering on their action plan.

10. **Start and finish on a positive note**. Highlight the benefits for the performer in undertaking the agreed action plan between coaching sessions.

Avoid the following feedback traps:

• Making suggestions without asking, e.g. "If I were you what I would do is . . ."

• Stating opinions, not facts

• Trying to improve more than one thing at a time

- Giving only bad news — emphasise the positive

- Telling

- Making sweeping statements and generalisations

- Comparing performance to that of other people

- Not giving examples

- Not giving regular feedback

- Not giving feedback soon after the observed behaviour.

Check out that feedback has been received:

- Are they smiling?

- Are they making eye contact?

- Do they look puzzled or angry?

- Do they want to discuss the next steps?

- Are they looking withdrawn or concerned?

- Are they making notes and recording actions?

- Can they summarise the key points?

**Feedback Questions**

*A Five-step Feedback Format*

- **Q1: Ask what worked**. By finding out what the performer thinks first using a questioning approach, you allow them the opportunity to discover for themselves what was positive in the performance. By beginning with a "What worked?" question, you're showing that you value the positive aspects of the performance. This approach will also help the performer and coach to tune in on the same wavelength and to build rapport.

- **Q2: Ask what didn't work**. Having asked what worked, it is now easier to manage defensiveness about what didn't work. By keeping the conversation focused on the process you help the performer to reduce self-doubt and fear of criticism. The focus is on improvement, not blame. Concentrate on specifics and look for examples of observed behaviour.

- **Q3: Ask what they might do differently next time**. This question opens the way for the performer to look at actionable points that require improvement. Keep the performer focused on changing just one to three parts of the performance. If you go for more, then the performer may become overwhelmed.

- **Q4: Offer to give your own observations**. "Would you like any further suggestions from me?" By not jumping in at the beginning with your observations, you have allowed your relationship to become a partnership. This question will probably be met by "yes" because the performer is keen to learn what you might be able to add to *their* thinking. Address those points that have been analysed by the performer. If you have further points written down, try to keep them for another session. Remember, if there are several areas of improvement, you don't eat the elephant in one sitting.

- **Q5: Work out an agreement**. Ask the performer to propose a solution; if necessary, you then propose your own. Agree upon an explicit action plan. Check understanding and commitment. Ask them to summarise their action points. Ensure both of you write these points down in your respective logs. Agree your next review date and time.

## Types of Feedback

There are four types of feedback:

1. Silence

2. Criticism (negative)

3. Advice

4. Reinforcement (positive).

*Silence*:

- Can decrease confidence

- Reduces performance in the long term

- Gives people no benchmark

- Creates problems when performance is low and reviews are held

- Can make people feel insecure.

*Criticism (negative)*:

- Produces excuses

- Rarely gets at the root cause of low performance

- Causes resentment (you never catch me doing things right)

- Decreases confidence and self-esteem

- Leads to avoidance of meetings and discussions.

*Advice*:

- Can sometimes be ignored, or a poor result following an advisory session can be blamed on you

- If delivered sensitively can improve confidence

- Can improve the relationship

- Can increase performance

- In all cases advice should be accompanied by examples and observations.

*Reinforcement (positive)*:

- Positive reinforcement is the best form of feedback

- Increases confidence

- Increases performance

- Increases motivation

- Encourages people to try new tasks and take risks

- Reinforces positive behaviour, which should result in repetition of the positive action.

## The Feedback Loop

The review process may show that some of your original goals
and objectives need to be revised or you may even wish to re-
consider the whole value of the coaching process if you are en-
countering non-co-operation over a period of time. The review
process should therefore feed back into the earlier phases of
the coaching process so that the process adapts to the individual needs and achievements of the performer (see Figure 21).

*Figure 21*

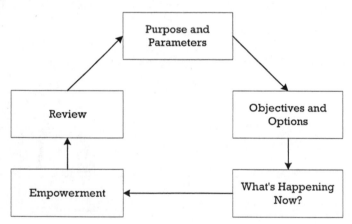

The review makes the process never-ending, which is what you
want — remember, no one's so good they can't get better. Each
new coaching session begins with the purpose and parameters.
After the first coaching session, each subsequent purpose and
parameters section in the coaching session should begin with a
review of the last meeting.

# Chapter 11

# Keeping Records

*"If it isn't written down, it didn't happen."*

The POWER coaching model is a framework for performance enhancement, and it is underpinned by record keeping. So where do you write things down? In the following pages we have assembled a number of forms that you may want to use as they are, or adapt for your own organisation.

### Form 1 — A Blank Piece of Paper

The easiest thing to use for note-taking, either during a coaching discussion or especially during an observation (part of What is Happening Now), is a blank sheet of paper. You might want to divide the paper into two columns — the left side to record the discussion or the observation, and the right column to record items that can be measured for improvement. Your note-taking, which records the discussion or observation, is very important for helping both of you to review and analyse afterwards what actually happened. If you have shorthand, that's a bonus, otherwise through practice and acting like a court clerk, you'll be able to record what was said. Capture the content of the discussion or observation first and analyse it afterwards.

For example, the salesperson might say that they want to improve their closing technique. You would write that down on the left side of the page. If you believe that improving closing technique would improve their performance and could be measured, draw an arrow from this to the right side. When it comes to reviewing the discussion, it should focus you on how you might measure the effectiveness of improving closing technique. Even if it doesn't improve it, you will have identified something that doesn't work, which is better than not knowing at all.

## Form 2 — Improvement Worksheet for the Salesperson

This form could be completed by the performer as a preliminary exercise to setting out their coaching objectives.

| Performer | Date | Area | Coach |
|---|---|---|---|
| | | | |

**What am I trying to improve?**

**What's in it for me?**

**How will I know when I've succeeded?**

| Task | By when? | Whose help do I need? | What obstacles are there to overcome? |
|---|---|---|---|
| | | | |

## Form 3 — An Objective-Setting Focus Tool

This could be used by the salesperson before a coaching session to help them focus on their own goals prior to the discussion. In POWER, this is O, which helps the performer to identify their coaching objectives.

1. What do I want to achieve?

2. How is this my own goal and not someone else's?

3. If this is part of a bigger goal, what's the big picture?

4. What will be the payoff for me in achieving this goal and how will I feel about it?

5. When do I want to achieve this by?

6. How realistic is this?

7. Whose help do I need?

8. How will I go about getting that help?

9. What have I done about achieving my goal so far?

10. What have been the results?

11. What have been the obstacles?

12. How could I have done it differently?

13. What can I do now to move closer to my goal?

14. On a scale of one to ten, what is the likelihood of success?

## Form 4 — Analysing Performance in Behavioural Detail

The coach can use this form as part of helping to identify What is Happening Now.

| Performer | Area | Coach |
|---|---|---|
| *Behaviour* | | *Analysis* |
| Date | Write down a description of the behaviour you have observed. Give specific examples and don't make assumptions. | Decide whether the behaviour is good or bad. Is it knowledge, skill or attitude based? |
| | | |
| | | |
| | | |
| | | |

## Form 5 — A Continuous Development Plan

This form can be used as part of empowering the performer to take ownership of their own development.

| Performer | Area | Coach |
|---|---|---|
| | | |

| | Action Agreed | Review |
|---|---|---|
| Date | What have you both agreed to do, by when and with what result? | What happened, and what is the next stage? |
| | | |
| | | |
| | | |
| | | |
| | | |

## Form 6 — A Training Course Assessment

This could be used as a mechanism of feedback to you after one of your salespeople has attended a central training event. It will help to ensure that the knowledge and skills acquired on the course are being transferred back to the job.

Salesperson _____

Course _____ Date _____

| Objectives: | Tick or Cross |
|---|---|
| 1. Introduced themselves to the customer in role play in a confident manner and one which complies with the company's sales process | |
| 2. Explained the need to sit in front of the sales visuals and delivered the script confidently | |
| 3. Arranged the seating positions so that the customer(s) could see the visuals effectively | |
| 4. All of this was done in a manner to promote professionalism and which would ensure that the company's message would be delivered in the best possible conditions | |
| Etc | |

Where an "X" is shown what prevented it from being achieved?

_____

_____

Remedial training required:

| Description | Suggested method (on-the-job training or central course) | Deadline |
|---|---|---|
| | | |

Confirmation of remedial action to achieve satisfactory level of competence:

## Form 7 —Empowerment Worksheet

This could be used both by the coach and the salesperson setting out agreed area(s) for improvement. On completion, it could be attached to the POWER form 8 if appropriate.

| Performer | Area | Coach | Date |
|---|---|---|---|
|  |  |  |  |

| What are we trying to improve? | | |
|---|---|---|
| Knowledge | Solution | Examples |
|  |  |  |
| Skill | Solution | Examples |
|  |  |  |
| Motivation | Solution | Examples |
|  |  |  |

## Form 8 — The POWER Record

This is a permanent record of either an observation or a meeting. Copies should be given to the salesperson to keep and produce at each subsequent meeting. You should complete this immediately after each coaching session.

| Performer | Area | Coach | Date |
|---|---|---|---|
| | | | |

(P) What is the purpose of this observation/meeting for the coach?

(O) What objective(s) is the performer hoping to achieve?

(W) What is the current situation/what happened during the observation/what was discussed?

(E) What action/step/improvement does the performer have to take? What assistance will the coach provide?

(R) When will this be reviewed?

## A Champion's Journal Example

This Champion's Journal is intended to be your personal log for the training and development that you undertake during the champion's programme. This diary also allows you to record activities or achievements that you take pride in and which are important to you in reaching your own personal goals and ambitions. The sections of the journal can be used to record incidents where you felt you learned something that was important to you. This journal is yours to keep. You must choose whether it's important and valid for you to check where you're going in terms of your performance. It's worth remembering that if you don't write your goals down, how can you check that they remain what you want? Equally, if you don't log your successes, the development needs you have and the positive changes that will result, how can you be positive that you have achieved them? Sometimes it can be comforting to us all to be able to remind ourselves of our ability to achieve and our willingness to learn through looking back at the written word.

**Sessions** _____ **Date** _____

What was it about?

What did I learn?

How can I apply this to my job?

Further development I should undertake:

# Chapter 12

# The Coach in Action

*"Strive for excellence not perfection."*
— H. Jackson Brown Jr.

This chapter focuses on a number of vignettes taken from actual case studies in which the POWER coaching model has been used. We have changed the names of the players, but the situations are real. We will show how coaching has enhanced performance in a number of roles, not just sales. Also explained will be the Metacoach role, i.e. the person who coaches the coach.

## Vignette No. 1 — Learning to Use a Spreadsheet

As computers are being increasingly used in the sales workplace, helping salespeople master the mysteries of spreadsheets and databases can sometimes be a challenge. Nearly all forms of computer systems training leave performers bemused and trainers frustrated. Within an hour, most performers are totally confused and trainers are usually oblivious that the lights have gone out. Over the last seven years, we have evaluated numerous computer training events across a multitude of companies and can guarantee that current practices in computer systems training for initial non-users are in many cases a total waste of time and money. The problem most trainers are faced with is that computer systems change so rapidly, and therefore the tendency is to employ external agents to carry out training. It is not uncommon to find that these trainers, whilst vaguely competent in the software package, are usually the worst trainers. In addition, the way in which they work demands that training sessions are most likely to be a full day at a minimum. If you examine the success of these events, you will find that most people learn little after the first hour.

Before moving on to coaching in computer systems, we strongly recommend that you adopt some basic rules for computer training, which should be:

- **Rule 1. Each training event should last no more than one hour**. For most people, more than one hour's computer training produced something akin to brain death.

- **Rule 2. The first event should not proceed until the trainer has drawn up plans to test understanding and competence after each hour**. We found that if trainers were to test for Rule 2 after each hour has passed, they would be amazed at how little has sunk in. Instead, most computer systems trainers drone on for hours, oblivious to an increasingly comatose audience. The coach can't begin coaching until performers have reached a level of basic competence (the line of acceptable performance), but then having done so, the effect can be dramatic in reinforcing and embedding learning.

- **Rule 3. The coach should resist telling the performer what to do**. In this case study the performer had received some training but wasn't progressing very well and the manager was concerned that perhaps the individual wasn't suited to operating computer-based systems, although he was a good salesperson.

*Coach*: The first thing we need to agree is the purpose of this first meeting.

*Performer*: Well, it's to learn to use the spreadsheet.

*Coach*: Is it to learn to use the spreadsheet or is it to decide how to go about learning to use it?

*Performer*: My boss says I've to learn about it.

*Coach*: How long has he given you?

*Performer*: He just says that he needs me to use this new spreadsheet as soon as possible.

*Coach*: And what's the reason for that?

*Performer*: The new budgetary controls and forecasts all work on this.

*Coach*: And what would be the effect of your becoming competent in using the system?


For the sake of brevity we have cut down the length of this introduction, but some of these initial discussions can be tortuous, the reason being that in most cases people don't volunteer to undertake new systems training. Generally, they are told that a new system is being introduced and that they have to learn it. We have conducted field trials on the traditional method of learning and compared it to the coaching style. In each case, people learned more rapidly, were more competent, and output a higher quality and quantity of work using the coaching model. In this particular case, as in so many others, training can often be seen as an intrusion, something that performers are forced to undertake and therefore their acceptance and learning is impaired. What we were looking to do here was to make the performer find a personal benefit which could be moulded into a personal goal.

*Performer*: It would get him off my back, for one thing.

*Coach*: And would that be of benefit?

*Performer*: It certainly would. He's a bit of tyrant if we don't get things right.

*Coach*: So what will you feel like when you can demonstrate your competence to him?

*Performer*: I'll feel a lot better. I don't seem to be getting to grips with it at all.

*Coach*: So, John, the purpose then of this meeting is to prepare a plan that will enable you to use the spreadsheet competently within four weeks so that you can help your boss to produce the budgetary forecasts for the finance department each month end.

*Performer*: Yes, that sounds good, when do I start?

*Coach*: Well, first thing we need to agree is whether that's possible, and what my role is.

*Performer*: I suppose it's possible. Other people are doing it, and your role is to teach me. I've already received basic training but I haven't really applied what I learned on the course. In fact I'm a bit confused about what I've covered on the course.

*Coach*: Well, perhaps we should set a goal of finding out whether it's possible by reviewing progress at the end of this session. So far as my role as teacher is concerned, you've had teaching before, and yet it doesn't seem to have sunk in. Is that fair?

*Performer*: Yes, I suppose so. Maybe the last trainer wasn't very good.

*Coach*: That could very well be the case. What else could have been the problem?

*Performer*: I suppose you want me to say that I wasn't a very good pupil.

*Coach*: I don't want you to say anything that you don't want to. All I'm interested in is to examine a range of alternative reasons and possible options for a solution.

*Performer*: OK. It might have been me.

*Coach*: Anything else?

*Performer*: I don't think so.

*Coach*: I've thought of something that might have contributed if you are interested in exploring it.

*Performer*: Yes, what is it?

*Coach*: What about the way in which your training was arranged? Were you comfortable with it?

*Performer*: Well, not really. It all happened a bit too quickly. There was too much to take in and by the end of the day I was totally confused.

*Coach*: So what could we do that would make you feel more comfortable?

*Performer*: Take it more slowly, and let me practise each part of the system until I get it right before going on.

*Coach*: Are there any problems with that?

*Performer*: It will take a long time.

*Coach*: So what are the benefits?

*Performer*: At least I won't forget it.

*Coach*: And what will you feel about doing it right?

*Performer*: I'll feel more confident.

*Coach*: And how do you think you'll approach the next lesson?

*Performer*: I'll probably be better at it, and might even do it more quickly.

*Coach*: So what else could you do to speed it up?

*Performer*: I could practise more often.

*Coach*: And when could you do that?

*Performer*: Whenever I get the chance during the day.

*Coach*: Anything else?

*Performer*: Well I suppose I could stay back for a while and practise after work.

*Coach*: Is that what you want to do?

*Performer*: Not really.

*Coach*: So what will be the effect of not practising?

*Performer*: I'll be no further forward.

*Coach*: What have you actually done about it so far?

*Performer*: You mean about learning to use it? Not a lot.

*Coach*: And the result of that?

*Performer*: I'm no better at it.

*Coach*: What were the obstacles?

*Performer*: Nothing really, just me. I didn't see why I had to practise in my own time for something I didn't bring into the department.

*Coach*: And now?

*Performer*: I can see there's something in it for me.

*Coach*: And what do you feel about it?

*Performer*: I'm ready to give it a go.

Although it may seem like a long process, the benefit here for us was that we now had a performer with a totally different attitude towards learning, and the battle appeared almost won without even touching the keyboard. As in all things concerned with performance enhancement, the key is in the mind.

*Coach*: Now, please put the spreadsheet up on the screen. You've told me that this is as far as you reached last time before things started going wrong.

*Performer*: Well the trainer ran through some of the buttons I had to press but I forgot which ones. I have to keep switching the thing off to get back to the start.

*Coach*: What is it you want to do?

*Performer*: I want to prepare a forecast for the month's sales.

*Coach*: How do you think you might do that?

*Performer*: I suppose I type the figures in that column.

*Coach*: How will you know which month they relate to?

*Performer*: I need to have the months at the top of the columns.

*Coach*: Then do it.

The performer typed in the words, putting spaces between the months. However, as he did not "tab" between columns, the words gathered together in one column, and eventually as the column width was used up, disappeared.

*Coach*: So what's happening?

*Performer*: I don't know. The words are at the bottom of the screen but they don't appear in the column.

*Coach*: What is it you want to do?

*Performer*: I want to put a separate month in each column.

*Coach*: How were you trying to move from column to column?

*Performer*: I pressed the space bar.

*Coach*: And what happened?

*Performer*: It just put a space into the column.

*Coach*: Which other key could you press to jump to the next column?

*Performer*: The tab?

*Coach*: Do it then and let's see what happens.

*Performer*: The cursor moved to the next column.

*Coach*: So what will you do next time when you what to move between columns?

*Performer*: I'll press the tab key.

*Coach*: What do you want to do next?


As we progressed, the performer learned more in 20 minutes than he had learned in days. In reality, he had learned how to use the spreadsheet, but was unable to apply that learning. This is a very simple example of part of a coaching process that taught someone to learn how to use a spreadsheet in a fraction of the time that traditional learning methods would. For any coach using this method, it may appear very slow over the first few lessons, but it will become evident that the performer retains far more information and becomes more competent than it would normally take. In this particular case, John managed to become an accomplished user of a number of systems. It improved his confidence, which in turn had a beneficial effect on his results.

### Vignette No. 2 — Gaining Sales Appointments by Telephone

Sheila is a life insurance salesperson. She recently attended a sales course where she was taught to use a particular sales script that had been found to be effective. When she started in the field, her appointment rate was very poor, which was put down to her inability to get client appointments by telephone. She was now in danger of not surviving past her probationary period. As in the last vignette, we had covered the purpose of the session, and what we felt we were able to achieve within the timescale.

*Coach*: What's the long-term goal from contacting this person?

*Performer*: To sell them some life insurance.

*Coach*: What will stop that from happening?

*Performer*: Well for a start they might not want to see me.

*Coach*: Does that happen often?

*Performer*: Quite a lot.

*Coach*: Why is that?

*Performer*: I don't know. They just don't want insurance.

*Coach*: Is that what you're asking for?

*Performer*: No. I ask for an appointment to see them.

*Coach*: So it's the appointment they turn down, is it?

*Performer*: I suppose so.

*Coach*: Before we progress, you need to decide what it is that they're objecting to.

*Performer*: I don't know.

*Coach*: Are you using the telephone sales script you were given?

*Performer*: Yes.

*Coach*: Say it to me.

The performer repeated her version of the script, which as it turned out wasn't the same one she had been supplied with.

*Coach*: It's not the same as the one we developed last time.

*Performer*: It didn't work.

*Coach*: How often did it not work?

*Performer*: I don't know. I tried it a few times and it didn't work.

*Coach*: So you changed it.

*Performer*: Yes.

*Coach*: And what happened?

*Performer*: It still doesn't work.

*Coach*: What do you think the reason is?

*Performer*: They still don't want insurance.

*Coach*: Can we go back to the beginning? What is it you want from me?

In some cases, performers can be hostile to change and any implied criticism. It can be frustrating for the coach to be faced with someone who appears to lack any positive intention of learning, but the coach needs to be patient and to focus on his or her coaching performance at this stage, not the reticence of the performer. We pursued the point.

*Performer*: Well, I'm not getting any appointments. I think it's more to do with the fact that business is tight at the moment rather than my style. I've done what you said, but it doesn't work.

*Coach*: Just a minute. At the moment, the script you developed doesn't work. Others using the same script are making it work. Let me hear you say the script we gave you.

The performer repeated her own version. We asked her to say it again three more times.

*Coach*: It's different every time.

*Performer*: Well, it's flexible. It depends on what the prospect says.

*Coach*: But not only am I the same person listening, I also haven't said anything yet.

It took some time but the performer eventually realised that she didn't have a script and the request for the appointment depended entirely on how she felt at the time. Considering that getting appointments by telephone is most salespeople's *bête noir,* she usually felt very negative and nervous about making telephone calls — hence the poor response.

*Coach*: I want you to use the script.

There are times when the coach has to impose a regime. It's pointless allowing people to run the 100 metres in whatever direction they like — they would be disqualified. When you coach a football team, there are rules about the area of play and the time allowed in each half. In some sales situations, and this is the part most salespeople and managers resist, there may be rules, like a script, which have to be enforced. We had already proven, by using this particular scripting method, that the appointment rates for other salespeople had increased dramatically. In some cases, it had helped to move people from a 20 per cent strike rate to 80 per cent within one session. If, as a coach, you have prescribed something that works generally as part of the initial training programme, which was the case here, and people who choose to ignore it haven't found a better way of doing it, which again was the situation here, the coach can insist on imposing what was agreed at the training stage before going on.

*Coach*: I want you to use the script and I'm going to watch you, listen to you, and record your performance.

In this scenario it became apparent to the performer that her performance was so poor that even those wanting to buy insurance would not give her an appointment. We insisted she keep practising the same script, playing it back to her each time. Each time it sounded better. Within an hour of adopting the script and having her performance coached, she was achieving high levels of success on the telephone.

### Vignette No. 3 — Training the Trainer

Peter is a sales training consultant. He writes and delivers training events to all levels of salespeople. Whilst an accomplished writer, his delivery style was very stilted, so much so that the response he used to get from course delegates was less than favourable. We watched his presentations on a number of occasions and although we found them to be technically accomplished, they lacked something. We noticed that Peter wrote all of his notes out in minute detail prior to delivering a session. During a session he would have his notes in front of him, meticulously typed up and laid out so that he could see them. As soon as he moved away from his notes, however, he looked and sounded ill at ease.

We remembered some time ago telling him to forget his notes and deliver from slides. It is the style we use ourselves when delivering training or making speeches at conferences or seminars. We put the slides together first, then write up a script, and then deliver from the slides. The advice had gone unheeded.

*Coach*: Peter, I've got thirty minutes now. How can we best utilise the time?

*Performer*: I'd like you to help me sort out this problem with my
delivery. I just can't get it right.

*Coach*: In thirty minutes it might not be possible to do a complete job. Can I suggest that you present your latest session to
me? I'll watch it, and record it. We can have a brief discussion,
after which I want you to watch the video playback, and tell me
what you see.

Peter agreed. We arranged for a couple of people to attend the
session. His presentation took 15 minutes, and sure enough,
during it, whilst he stayed near his notes everything went well.
As soon as he ventured out of sight of his notes it became lack-
lustre. The problem was also that, even when in sight of his
notes, because he kept looking down, the whole presentation
lacked impact. After the others had left, we discussed it.

*Coach*: What did you feel?

*Performer*: I don't know. It was all right, but it wasn't great.

*Coach*: What were you trying to do?

*Performer*: I was attempting to impart some knowledge.

*Coach*: Anything else?

*Performer*: I suppose I was trying to motivate people to learn.

*Coach*: Did you achieve that?

*Performer*: I don't think so.

*Coach*: How do you know?

*Performer*: I didn't feel good, and they didn't look particularly
inspired.

We had been rewinding the tape, and began playing it back with the volume switched off.

*Coach*: Where didn't you feel comfortable?

*Performer*: What do you mean?

*Coach*: You say you didn't feel good. By that do you mean comfortable?

*Performer*: Yes.

*Coach*: So where wasn't it comfortable?

*Performer*: I don't know. Do you mean physically?

*Coach*: Yes.

*Performer*: I suppose round about here. [He pointed to his shoulder.]

*Coach*: Look at the playback, and tell me what's happening.

A video can be a very useful tool, especially if used correctly. We find it extremely useful to turn the sound off on playback, as the noise can be distracting. In most cases, what you want to focus on are the body movements. In a case like this, they tell you more about performance than the words that are used.

*Performer*: I don't look too happy.

*Coach*: What else?

*Performer*: I look uncomfortable.

*Coach*: All the time?

*Performer*: No, just some of the time.

*Coach*: When in particular?

*Performer*: When I'm standing near the desk. And when I return to my desk.

*Coach*: What about when you move away from the desk?

*Performer*: It looks all right.

*Coach*: So what is there about the desk?

*Performer*: It's where the overhead projector is.

*Coach*: How do you look when you're changing the slides?

*Performer*: OK.

*Coach*: So what else is there on the desk?

*Performer*: My notes are on it. [Peter began to laugh.]

*Coach*: What are you laughing at?

*Performer*: You're going to tell me it's the notes, you've told me that before.

*Coach*: I'm not going to tell you anything. What do you do when you stand at the desk and when you return to the desk?

*Performer*: I look at my notes.

*Coach*: And what happens?

*Performer*: I look unhappy. But I'm not, you see. I'm only studying my notes.

*Coach*: I understand. But what do you look like?

*Performer*: Unhappy.

*Coach*: And what effect is it having on the audience?

*Performer*: It makes them unhappy.

*Coach*: So what else could you do?

*Performer*: I could smile.

*Coach*: What else?

*Performer*: I could look at them more.

*Coach*: What will that mean?

*Performer*: I won't be able to do both. I mean I can't look at them and my notes.

*Coach*: What else could you do?

*Performer*: I could learn my notes. But I might forget something.

*Coach*: Will they know?

*Performer*: I don't suppose so.

*Coach*: When do you look happy?

*Performer*: When I'm standing in the front of the table. Except for that part.

*Coach*: What happened there?

*Performer*: I forgot about something and went back to the table to look at my notes.

*Coach*: If you're interested, I could suggest another way of looking at it, but it's up to you if you want to explore it.

*Performer*: Yes.

*Coach*: Could it be that you didn't forget something as much as remembered that your notes were on the table?

[Peter began to laugh again.]

*Coach*: So what do you want to do?

*Performer*: I want to try it again without my notes.

*Coach*: When?

*Performer*: Now.

We asked Peter to do his presentation again a few more times. We left him to record himself, playing it back each time and looking at his performance. We had run out of time, but we did agree that later on we would watch him again. By then he had improved immensely. He is now a very accomplished speaker and continues to improve.

## Vignette No. 4 — Using the Coaching Model as a Performance Appraisal Tool

Using the POWER model is not restricted to performance improvement in a skills sense. It can also be used for interviewing and for appraisals. Here is an example of how we have used it for the latter.

Margaret was a sales administrator. Her last boss told us that she just came to work to socialise, and showed little aspiration for doing anything else. When we examined her previous appraisals, her work appeared to be reasonable, but everyone had the feeling that she could do a lot better.

*Coach*: Margaret, tell me what you want out of this discussion.

*Performer*: It's the yearly appraisal, isn't it?

*Coach*: That could be my purpose, but what's in it for you?

*Performer*: If I get a good appraisal, I get a bigger rise.

*Coach*: What else do you want?

*Performer*: I'd like to know what's expected of me. What I'm supposed to do to get on.

*Coach*: What are you keen to do?

*Performer*: Well, I don't want to stay a sales administrator assistant forever.

*Coach*: So what do you want from me?

*Performer*: I suppose I want you to tell me how to get up the ladder.

*Coach*: So what do you have to do to get promoted?

*Performer*: Be in the right place at the right time.

*Coach*: Anything else?

*Performer*: Do a good job.

*Coach*: Is that what you want?

*Performer*: How do you mean? Do a good job, or get promoted?

*Coach*: Both.

*Performer*: I suppose they both go together.

*Coach*: Do they go together as far as you're concerned, or is that the way it works around here?

*Performer*: That's difficult. I've seen people do a good job and not get promoted, and I've seen some people who don't do a good job get promoted.

*Coach*: So which is it for you?

*Performer*: I'd like to do both.

*Coach*: So is this a long-term goal of yours, promotion, or is it part of a greater plan?

*Performer*: I'd like to think I could manage the department at some time. It might not sound likely, but I think I'm capable.

*Coach*: What's not so likely about it?

*Performer*: Well, it doesn't depend on me does it?

*Coach*: Who does it depend on then?

*Performer*: Well, people like you for a start.

*Coach*: So what would make people like me consider you for promotion?

*Performer*: If I did a good job?

*Coach*: Anything else?

*Performer*: I don't know.

*Coach*: What about making people like me aware of your management aspirations?

*Performer*: What do you mean?

*Coach*: I notice from your file that there's no mention of management aspirations.

*Performer*: I didn't mention it before.

*Coach*: And what do you feel was the consequence of that?

*Performer*: Perhaps people thought I wasn't interested.

*Coach*: So what could you do differently?

*Performer*: Talk about it.

*Coach*: Anything else?

*Performer*: Ask for help.

*Coach*: In what way?

*Performer*: Well, what do I have to do?

*Coach*: Can I just check something out first? Is it management you want, just promotion, or is there something else?

*Performer*: I don't really know. I don't want to be doing this job forever.

*Coach*: So is it not wanting to be in this job forever, or the fact that you want to manage other people?

*Performer*: Not particularly, but it seems that it's the only way to get on.

*Coach*: What do you mean by getting on? What is there about getting on that appeals to you?

*Performer*: I want to feel useful, looked up to, recognised for doing something worthwhile, something important.

We have observed a great many appraisals over the years. Most are part of the endless paper chase that goes on in organisations, and most eventually lead to arranging for mindless training sessions which simply fill out the requirement that managers have to satisfy agreed training needs at the yearly appraisal. Thousands of people are on management development programmes as a result of poorly conducted appraisals, where it's assumed that everybody and his brother wants to be in management. People simply want to get through the appraisal interview. The answer to most appraisals is usually whatever the training course prospectus contains. We once included an assertiveness training module in a course prospectus for VDU operators, just to see what would happen. After the appraisals had been conducted, we had a 97 per cent take-up for assertiveness training. The subject had never come up on any previous appraisal. We couldn't work out why VDU operators wanted assertiveness training, other than to perhaps get away from the VDU. We eventually owned up and cancelled the module and nobody complained. Perhaps they did need assertiveness training after all.

*Coach*: Margaret, is there anything else that you could do apart from management?

*Performer*: I thought about computer programming, but I can't do it.

*Coach*: What do you mean you can't do it?

*Performer*: I don't know of anybody who got promoted internally to be a computer programmer. They get them all from the outside.

*Coach*: Is that what you want to do?

*Performer*: I'm interested in computers. All I seem to do here though is word processing.

*Coach*: So what have you done about it before now?

*Performer*: Nothing.

*Coach*: And what was the result?

*Performer*: Nothing.

*Coach*: So what could you do?

*Performer*: Do something about it.

*Coach*: Such as what?

*Performer*: I don't know.

*Coach*: First thing is, is to decide why you want to do it, and then we can work out what to do. Why do it?

*Performer*: It's something I'm really interested in.

*Coach*: What is there about it?

*Performer*: Well I know Carol in computer programming, and she really seems to enjoy her job.

*Coach*: So is it enjoying your job that's important, or having aspirations to be a computer programmer?

*Performer*: That's difficult. It's just that her job looks more interesting than mine. It looks more complicated, and pays more.

*Coach*: Is it the complexity of the job that interests you, or the higher pay?

*Performer*: It probably goes back to what I was saying before, about being recognised, feeling valued.

*Coach*: Do you feel valued now?

*Performer*: No, not really.

*Coach*: What's the problem?

*Performer*: Well, every day just seems the same. I don't seem to be getting anywhere.

*Coach*: So what could you do about it?

*Performer*: I could change jobs.

*Coach*: Yes, we've looked at that. What else could you do?

*Performer*: I don't know.

*Coach*: What about changing this job?

*Performer*: What do you mean?

*Coach*: What could you do about the content of this job that would make it more challenging?

*Performer*: I've never really thought about it.

*Coach*: Surely there's something about it or the department that you've thought you could do better, or change.

*Performer*: We don't appear to be able to provide managers with the answers they want without a real panic going on. It takes ages and everybody gets a bit distraught with the pressure when there's a rush on to provide some information for the month end returns.

*Coach*: So what could you do about it?

*Performer*: Nothing really. The information isn't easily accessible.

*Coach*: What would make it accessible?

*Performer*: A computer database for a start, but we haven't got one.

*Coach*: Do you think it's a good idea?

*Performer*: Yes, I do.

*Coach*: So what could you do about it?

*Performer*: I could find out about one.

*Coach*: Is that what you want to do?

*Performer*: I wouldn't mind. It would be quite interesting.

*Coach*: What obstacles do you see in the way?

*Performer*: Cost, probably.

*Coach*: So what could you do about it?

*Performer*: Prove it was saving money.

*Coach*: How confident do you feel about doing it then?

*Performer*: Pretty good. I think I'd like to have a go.

*Coach*: What else would doing this project do for you?

*Performer*: It might give me an insight into computers a bit more.

*Coach*: And management?

*Performer*: Yes, it probably would.

*Coach*: What support do you want from me?

*Performer*: I'd need some help on where to start, and perhaps you could tell me how much we've got in the budget so that I know how far to go.

*Coach*: Do it then.

Margaret successfully investigated a database for the statistics we needed for the month end reports. She enjoyed it so much that she went on to implement a number of improvements to the department, part of which was to train other people in adopting the new systems. She didn't become a computer programmer but became a computer trainer instead. She tells us she loves the freedom of the job, and the last thing she wants is to be a manager.

## Vignette No. 5 — Coaching Managers: The Role of the Metacoach

The Metacoach is the coach of the coach. Even the coach needs feedback, and similarly the POWER model can be used to give that internal feedback on the coach's performance. The problem you may face with managers is their reluctance to be coached at coaching. A good way to set this up is to arrange a session which involves a physical activity so that all concerned can "feel" the effect of being coached, and of being coached as a coach.

One way that works is either to take managers to a golf driving range, arrange for a golf session indoors using a net, or to buy some of those small plastic balls, the size of golf balls, which are hollow and have holes in the sides. These can still be hit quite hard, but they don't inflict any damage when they hit anything. Obviously, if you are going to do this indoors, you'll need a large room with enough height to be able to swing a golf club. Place a screen five to ten yards away, or hang a large sheet from the ceiling. No matter how hard you hit the ball, the sheet or the screen will stop it.

Pick someone who has tried playing golf but isn't very good, and find an experienced player to coach them. Explain to the coach that you want them to coach the performer to hit the ball better. You then stand near the coach, and when appropriate call "time out" so that you can ask the coach the same coaching questions as are part of the model. The chances are that the experienced golfers won't be able to resist "telling" people what to do. The effect of you asking the POWER questions will help them realise what it's like to be coached, and what they are doing to the performer.

If the golf set-up is inappropriate, the same exercise can be achieved through playing snooker. Simplify the game by leaving just the cue ball and a few colours. Coaching sessions and metacoaching sessions can then be arranged. It is possible to go even further by standing another coach next to the metacoach, asking them what they are trying to achieve. Dependent upon the number of managers available, the metacoach role can be extended infinitely, and at times can result in both an enjoyable, humorous, and yet powerful learning experience. In fact, if you are training in a hotel which has a snooker table, using that can also help in straightforward coaching.

The following case study involves Alex who was a sales manager. He had been on a sales call with Sally, a salesperson who was performing on or around the acceptable performance line. After the call, Alex attempted to coach her to increase her performance next time. When observing the coaching session it was useful to take some notes using the POWER form shown in Chapter 11. It was also useful to get the coach to write down the benefits of the coaching session on a form similar to the one which is also included in Chapter 11. You may want to adapt this for everybody being coached.

*Coach*: What were you trying to achieve, Alex?

*Manager*: I was trying to get Sally to admit that she could have performed better on that last call.

*Coach*: Was that your purpose or hers?

*Manager*: Mine.

*Coach*: So what was her purpose?

*Manager*: I don't know.

*Coach*: So what's the problem?

*Manager*: You'll probably say that she won't be committed to a course of action if she isn't involved in setting out her own objectives.

*Coach*: OK. Let's go back to the purpose of the coaching session and the observation you made. What's the purpose of a coaching visit?

*Manager*: To improve the performance of the salesperson.

*Coach*: And how were you to achieve that?

*Manager*: By observing Sally on the call and providing her with feedback.

*Coach*: Good. What about you? What's the purpose of this session?

*Manager*: To help make me a better coach.

*Coach*: Is that your objective or mine?

*Manager*: Both, I suppose.

*Coach*: What will be the effect of making you a better coach?

*Manager*: The theory is that my people will perform better.

*Coach*: Is it theory or reality?

*Manager*: At the moment it's theory.

*Coach*: What's the difference with reality?

*Manager*: Well, up to now it hasn't worked.

*Coach*: What hasn't?

*Manager*: This coaching thing.

*Coach*: What specifically doesn't work?

*Manager*: I've been trying it for a few weeks now, and performance has stayed just the same.

*Coach*: So what could you do differently?

*Manager*: I could go back to doing what I was doing before.

*Coach*: Which was what?

*Manager*: Telling people, showing them, motivating them.

*Coach*: And how was that working?

*Manager*: All right.

*Coach*: What levels were people performing at?

*Manager*: About the same as now.

*Coach*: So what are you doing differently?

*Manager*: Coaching them.

*Coach*: Describe to me specifically what you did on this last session with Sally.

*Manager*: I got her to tell me what she was doing wrong.

*Coach*: How did you do that?

*Manager*: I got her to explain to me what she could have done better.

*Coach*: So what were you actually saying to her?

*Manager*: That she could have done something better.

*Coach*: What in particular did you focus on?

*Manager*: I asked her what there was about the way she opened the presentation that she could have done better.

*Coach*: What's the difference between telling her that the opening could have been better, and asking what there was about the opening that could have been better?

*Manager*: Well, she came up with the answer.

*Coach*: Alex, what was there about the opening few minutes of your coaching session that could have been handled better, allowing Sally to express herself before you manipulated her into saying that she could have done the opening better?

*Manager*: Just a minute. Are you saying that I didn't coach her properly in the opening few minutes?

*Coach*: Is that similar to what you did to Sally?

[There was a pause. The penny dropped.]

*Coach*: Alex, what was the result of this coaching session on Sally's next call?

*Manager*: It wasn't a great deal better.

*Coach*: And what have been the results of most of your coaching sessions with others?

*Manager*: I've already told you, not a lot has changed.

*Coach*: So what could you do differently?

*Manager*: OK, so I could try to ask the questions differently.

*Coach*: What in particular?

*Manager*: Let them express themselves more.

*Coach*: What effect would that have?

*Manager*: You'd say that it would commit them to change if they came up with it in the first place.

*Coach*: Let's say it actually had that effect, how would that make you feel?

*Manager*: I'd be happy if they improved.

*Coach*: What are you feeling at the moment?

*Manager*: Frustrated.

*Coach*: What about?

*Manager*: Well, I know what to say. It's just that . . .

*Coach*: Just what?

*Manager*: Sometimes it just doesn't come out right.

*Coach*: So what could you do about it?

*Manager*: Practise it more.

*Coach*: What support do you need?

*Manager*: I'd appreciate it if you continued to give me some feedback.

It took a few more sessions before John grasped the fact that he was manipulating responses, not empowering people. Obviously it would be impossible for you to coach all managers, but every now and then you have to step in and help. The ideal metacoach for the manager is the manager's line manager. If that isn't going to happen then you have to get yourself a coach somehow. We've known a number of sales managers who in the absence of senior manager involvement have set up a coaching support group for themselves, which sounds like a great idea.

*Coach*: John, let's have another look at the purpose of the coaching session with Sally. You said that the purpose of a coaching visit is to improve the performance of a salesperson. Does it matter how that improvement happens?

*Manager*: No, I suppose not.

*Coach*: Does it matter?

*Manager*: Only if she does something wrong which contravenes the rules.

*Coach*: And in that case what would you do?

*Manager*: I'd set out at the beginning what the rules were and how the game had to be played.

*Coach*: OK. So in the case of Sally, does she break the rules?

*Manager*: No.

*Coach*: So, as she's not exactly performing below the acceptable performance line, does it matter where the improvement comes from?

*Manager*: No.

*Coach*: Does this stop you from dictating the purpose of the coaching session?

*Manager*: No, I suppose not. The purpose for me remains to improve her performance.

*Coach*: And how often do you set this out as a general aim of your role as a coach?

*Manager*: I take it as read.

*Coach*: What else could you do?

*Manager*: I could talk about it more when I'm out with people.

*Coach*: Would that help?

*Manager*: It certainly wouldn't do any harm.

*Coach*: When else could you do it?

*Manager*: At sales meetings?

*Coach*: So when will you do that?

We agreed that John would revisit his vision at the next sales meeting and that we would observe him doing so and provide him with feedback. This coaching session resulted in John proposing that he might be manipulating people into providing him with the answers he wanted. He agreed to role-play having on-the-line performers set their own objectives, which was done until he sounded and appeared convincing. Within three months of this event, John had conducted another three coaching sessions and observations with Sally. The feedback from her was extremely positive and she became one of John's team who regularly exceeded target, providing John with the space he needed to improve the others in his team.

## Vignette No. 6 — Training Comes Before Coaching

We have presented extracts above on some coaching scenarios. Let's look briefly at two final case studies.

In the first case, a bank was concerned with the low customer take-up of serious illness cover by customers taking out mortgages. Following a training needs analysis with the loan advisors who sold the products, it became apparent that there were both training issues and coaching requirements.

Before looking at coaching, it was necessary in the first instance to address the training area. The training issues revolved around a lack of knowledge of the serious illness product. To help address these needs, a training video was put together with successful salespeople describing the product features and benefits together with simulated sales interviews with customers in which the product was successfully sold.

Training sessions were held using the sales training video together with some prepared sales scripts. Following the course, which involved sales role-plays, all loan advisors had specific action plans which they undertook to complete back on the job. Their sales managers undertook to sign off the loan advisors as competent when they satisfactorily role-played customer interviews using serious illness cover. When advisors were signed off as being able to demonstrate that they had reached an acceptable level of performance and started selling serious illness cover, the sales figures improved. However, the exercise had also highlighted that some advisors sold significantly more product than others. This is where coaching played its part.

Regional sales managers undertook to work with the loan advisors over a four-month period with the express purpose of developing their performance to higher levels beyond that reached by the training initiative. They followed the POWER coaching model with the performers. Following each coaching visit, the POWER form was completed and copies made. Improving performance was the agreed focus.

Some very positive results are now evident, including increased results of up to 26 per cent income. The feedback from customers has also been positive as they bought relevant products which addressed their security needs along with taking out mortgages. Reflecting on the success, one regional sales manager commented: "I always knew my sales staff had the potential to sell more products, but it was only by working in partnership with them, observing them in interviews, and by following a structured coaching approach that their confidence and competence grew."

## Vignette No. 7 — Managing a Performance Problem

When faced with a gap in work performance some sales managers automatically look for the employee to attend a training course. However, deeper analysis is required to discover the issue underlying the poor performance. It might be lack of training, but there might be some other cause.

The case study below highlights some of the areas which need to be looked at first where there is a performance gap before coaching is introduced. It also represents a useful checklist of questions to ask when confronted with a performance problem.

In our case, the sales manager was concerned that a certain salesperson was behind target and wasn't converting customer interviews into sales. She sought advice from us before sitting down with the salesperson. We went through the following checklist with her with regard to the performance gap.

We sought answers to the following questions:

- Is the salesperson aware that there is a performance gap? (If not make them aware of the gap.)

- Does the person have the necessary knowledge and skills to do the job? (If not provide appropriate training.)

- If the person has the knowledge and skills, have they done the job frequently? (If not provide them with the opportunities to undertake the job more regularly, as their skills might be rusty.)

In this instance the sales manager confirmed that the salesperson knew that there was a performance gap and that he had been well trained in both the classroom and on the job. We concluded from our assessment that it wasn't a training issue. We continued with our list of questions, trying to diagnose the full extent of the problem before offering a solution.

- Is the salesperson aware of the standards of performance required to successfully carry out the job?

- Does the salesperson understand his manager's expectations? If so, is he receiving regular feedback on his performance?

- Are the consequences of his performance clear?

(If the answer to these questions is No, these issues must be addressed in the first instance. For example, the salesperson must

be made aware of the benefits of good performance or the consequences of underperformance.)

- Are there any obstacles that stand in the way of good performance? (If there are any barriers to performance, such as
  lack of resources, authority, or time, these must be addressed and overcome.)

In our case study, following a discussion with the sales manager
using this checklist of questions, it became apparent that the
salesperson wasn't getting regular feedback from his sales
manager on his interview performance. Furthermore, the sales
manager agreed that she didn't have enough detail with regard
to how the sales interviews were conducted by the salesperson.
She couldn't put her finger on what the person was or wasn't
doing which prevented more sales. There was only one solution:
the sales manager had to spend time with the advisor in field interviews to see exactly what was going wrong. She agreed to
start coaching the salesperson over a two-month time frame and
agreed a specific date and time to sit in and observe the next
sales interview. The sales manager explained to the salesperson
that they would follow the POWER coaching template.

Over the ensuing two months, the sales manager coached
the salesperson. She pinpointed with the performer that in the
interview, although he asked some needs-based questions of
customers, he didn't feel comfortable or confident asking the
customer for the business. Following this coaching intervention
by the sales manager, the salesperson worked hard on the
agreed development action points and became stronger when
closing the sale. Results improved and the performance gap
was closed. The sales manager was very pleased with the enhanced performance. She reinforced the more assertive sales
behaviour displayed by the performer by praising them after
observing them in action with customers.

The sales manager confided to us that in the past she would
not have tolerated sub-standard performance for any length of
time and would have dismissed the salesperson. This new

managerial approach of coaching had worked and she intended to embrace it in her future dealings with her sales team.
While she didn't believe that it would work in every instance of
poor salesmanship, it certainly was a better approach than the
traditional management style she had previously used.

# Chapter 13

# Epilogue

*"The opponent inside one's head is more formidable than the one on the other side of the net."*
— Tim Gallwey

It has been said that to stop learning is to stop living. We are often asked if we can recommend something to read for people interested in coaching. Our feeling on this is that you should read anything and everything you can find on the subject. Even if after reading a complete book or article you gauge that there was nothing new or you didn't particular enjoy it, it is still worth the effort. People spend a great deal more time and energy feeding their bodies than their minds. Some people stretch their bodies to the limit in a vain attempt to stay young or healthy, and yet hardly ever consider how to keep their minds staying young and healthy. Just because you are trying to be a coach — and many of the analogies we use come from the athletics world — it doesn't mean that you have to also end up being a prime contender for a gold medal in the marathon. All things in moderation. However, your mental health will ultimately give you a great deal more pleasure and reward than the health of your body. The maxim "healthy mind in a healthy body" is all a matter of intensity. People have a tendency to vacillate towards a particular area of interest, and at times keeping physically fit and keeping mentally fit seem to be polarised. Given the choice, we probably choose the latter. If you can achieve a balance, so much the better, but if time is at a premium, and for most of us it is, then keep your mind alive. If you are driving a car you need petrol to keep it going. Similarly your mind drives you on and it needs fuel. Learning is to the mind what fuel is to the car.

The point about study is that, even if you don't appear to be taking it in, in it goes. The brain has an awesome capacity for recording information. Some communication experts may tell you that items that go into our short-term memory are eventually discarded. Only those that we store in our long-term memory can be recalled. When things happen, we don't make conscious decisions to put the experience in our short-term or long-term memory. Sometimes we remember them, sometimes we don't. It isn't memory that's the problem; it is recall. If we knew how, we could recall everything that has ever happened to us. Everything we have ever said, done, or seen is recorded; the problem is that we sometimes lose the key. There are those people who develop incredible recall processes, and we don't doubt that given the correct coaching we could all learn how to do it. In the meantime, why take the chance that you might miss something? Like us, from time to time you will have remembered something, but not where it came from. It came from a time when you read it, saw it or experienced it. If you fail to keep those experiences going, then you run the risk of closing down your ability to develop new ideas and new approaches.

If you can, put your studies on a formal footing. Take a prescribed course of study. If you already have a degree, take another one. The formality of academic study, at whatever level, can help maintain your impetus for self-improvement.

In terms of the job that we do, then the only recommendation we can make is that you focus on communication. It is communication that shapes the world. Stephen Hawking said, "Man's greatest achievements have come about through talking. Man's greatest failures have come about through not talking." It is a fact that the increase in communication over the last century has paradoxically reduced our ability to talk to each other. Part of this has to be that information is so readily available in visual form that people have lost the ability to find out things for themselves. Yet the volume of information available in written form is far greater than anything you will see on video or television.

**Vision, Visualisation, Self-esteem and Self-talk**

What is it that draws you to a particular person? There are those people who appear to attract followers, and yet why it happens remains a mystery. They appear to exude a confidence that is difficult to quantify but which has an effect on people they come into contact with. There are leaders who produce in their followers a sense of mission, of belonging, and a desire for achievement based on the needs for intrinsic reward. These people give reference to the achievements of the past, postulate a vision of the future, and influence action in the here and now. Charismatic leaders have vision. They seem to have the ability to get us to actually see the success of the future. They are few and far between.

In discussion with people who have achieved success in one form or another, a recurring theme was visualisation. People who are successful or who achieve something see it as a natural extension of their planning process. Success rarely comes as a surprise to the successful. They are geared up for it. They saw it some time ago and told themselves it would happen. It's an old conundrum: are people confident because they are successful, or are people successful because they are confident? Where does confidence come from? Some people will say it comes from within. If that's true, then we all have it. Perhaps some just hide it better than others. The Catch-22 of confidence is that it comes from other people who believe you're confident because you act confidently. It has to do with the conversations you have with yourself — your self-esteem.

Those people who have great self-esteem regularly tell themselves that they're on the journey to achieving their goals, and that they will succeed. In developing your coaching relationships with your salespeople, you will become a role model for their aspirations, not in terms of their personal goals but in the manner in which they approach it. Whilst motivation is a personal thing, your salespeople will be looking to you for inspiration. You can supply it by showing them how to feel confident in their own abilities. You do this by showing them how confident you are in your own. The feeling of your own self-worth is the single most important winning quality you can possess. It doesn't simply involve pride in what you have achieved, or even in what you intend to achieve, but a real joy in accepting who you are right now.

The biggest problem many people face is that they have no vision of the future. Your job is helping people develop that vision by expressing your own. The main reasons why people don't achieve their goals is that most aren't written down, and very few are verbally expressed. If you have a goal, write it down, and if you want your salespeople to achieve their goals, get them to write theirs down as well. In the process of writing down a goal it becomes evident that a goal statement alone is worthless. To achieve a goal, you have to know where you are now, where you want to be, and work out how to get there. Most people never write their goals down and as a consequence never begin the journey.

As a coach, you should keep and regularly update your own personal development plan. What are you trying to achieve as a coach? What knowledge, skills and behaviours do you need to adopt, and what level are you currently at? It will soon become apparent that you also need a coach, so get one. If you expect to sell the idea of coaching to others, then they will look to you for an example. If you demonstrate that you believe you know it all and don't need a coach, then they will assume the same of themselves.

A useful tool might be to use the format shown in Chapter 11. Complete your own personal plan before asking others to complete theirs, and if asked, share it with them. You should in any event have a development plan for each of your sales-people, and encourage them to keep their own records of achievement.

Lastly, get into the habit of seeing yourself achieve, and help your salespeople to see themselves achieving. It involves nothing simpler than closing your eyes and seeing yourself de-livering your best performance. Play the scene through in your mind until you can see, hear, feel and even smell the successful performance. If something goes wrong during this scene-setting, rewind and put it right until you see yourself delivering the perfect performance you want. Then repeat it as often as time allows before delivering the performance in reality. It is at this stage that fantasy and reality merge. The scene you have played through in your mind can and will happen.

## Words of Warning

As a coach, your effect on the performance of others can be dramatic. You could be the catalyst for immense change and for feelings of self-worth and achievement not previously experi-enced by the people you coach. It is at this stage that the rela-tionship you build of support and trust can become a crutch which, when you try to remove it, results in a collapse of per-formance and of self-confidence. At all times, you must ensure that people understand that their increase in performance has come from them and not from you. You are a facilitator, but you're not the reason for their newfound success.

Unless you develop in them a sense of their responsibility for performance and of their ability to sustain and improve that performance, then you could end up having to support them for life, and that just can't work.

Avoid trying to change people's personal lives. We know that your personal life can have an effect on your work per-formance, but that's a matter for people to resolve themselves, not for you as a coach to become enmeshed in. If you become involved in helping them to resolve personal issues, you will cross the boundary between a work coach and a personal counsellor and confidante. That is not to say that people won't want to see you as such and will attempt to share their personal problems, but where you can, avoid it. Coaching can be a draining experience, and you therefore need to focus on what you can and can't reasonably achieve. That is not to say that coaching techniques can't help people resolve their personal difficulties; it's just that, as an organisational coach, you can't be all things to all people. The biggest problem you will have is that in experiencing the power of coaching, in sensing your complicity in the achievement of others, and in the satisfaction of your own personal achievement, you will also be susceptible to believing that in some way all things are possible.

Your job is to give others the confidence to believe in their own ability to solve their own problems without you. Their confidence will come from the realisation that they have the ability to carry out a particular task you give them or that they have previously been unsuccessful at accomplishing. You need to give them a battle they can win so that they will go on to win bigger battles. Start with things they can do before giving them tasks they believe they can't accomplish. Your people may be disappointed if they fail along the way, but remember, in many cases they will stagnate or atrophy if they don't try.

Their confidence will come from their individual ability to do what is asked of them in their current roles, and this means high-quality induction training. Most people fail in new jobs not because they haven't got the ability, but because the induction training was lacking in sufficient direction and initial instruction about what was expected and how to do it. Make sure that, before you begin coaching someone to increased performance, they have received enough initial training.

Their confidence will come from others around them. Your job is to give the team a vision of collective achievement. Lastly, confidence comes from the fact that mistakes are tolerated. The best people you have will test the boundaries of your tolerance, and the tolerance of your company.

## Conclusion

Is coaching the answer we have all been looking for? We don't know. What we do know is that it is a better way to manage and to develop people than any other form of development we have yet seen or experienced. Yet if we are also to practise what we preach, then we will keep an open mind to the possibility of something else being developed that can be of use. In the meantime, we are convinced from experience that by adopting the process contained in this book, you too will experience the powerful effect of POWER coaching.

# Recommended Reading

Albrecht, Karl, *Brain Power*, Prentice Hall, 1980.

Bolt, Peter, *Coaching for Growth*, Oak Tree Press, 2000.

Brallier, Jess and Chabert, S., *Coach: A Treasury of Inspiration and Laughter*, Contemporary Books, 2000.

Bristol, Claude M., *The Magic of Believing*, Prentice Hall, 1985.

Burdett, John O., "To Coach, or Not to Coach — That is the Question!", *Industrial and Commercial Training*, Vol. 23, No. 5, 1991.

Buzan, Tony, *Use Your Head*, BBC Books, 1974.

Clarkson, Petruska, "Counselling, Psychotherapy, Psychology and Psychiatry", *Employee Counselling Today*, Vol. 3, No. 3, 1991.

Clutterbuck, D., *Learning Alliances*, Institute of Personnel and Development, 1998.

Dick, Frank, "Fitness to Win", *Target — Management Development Review*, Vol. 4, No. 3, MCB University Press, 1991.

Forster, Steve, "Hemery's Way", *Management Week*, 18 September 1991.

Fournies, Ferdinand, *Coaching for Improved Work Performance*, McGraw-Hill, 2000.

Freemantle, David, *The Stimulus Factor*, Prentice Hall, 2001.

Gallwey, Timothy W., *The Inner Game of Tennis*, Random House, 1975.

Gunnigle, Patrick (ed.), *The Irish Employee Recruitment Handbook*, Oak Tree Press, 1999.

Hemery, David, MBE, *Sporting Excellence: What Makes a Champion?* Collins Willow, 1991.

Hemery, David, MBE, "Sports Star Lessons for Managers", *Target — Management Development Review*, Vol. 4, No. 3, MCB University Press, 1991.

Hendricks W., *Coaching, Mentoring and Managing*, Career Press, 1996.

Henry, K., "The Introduction of Coaching as a Tool for Developing People in the Workplace", Dissertation (unpublished), part of MeD Degree, University of Sheffield, 2000.

James, Muriel and Jongeward, Dorothy, *Born to Win*, Addison-Wesley, 1971.

Maltz, Maxwell and Powers, Melvin, *Psycho-cybernetics*, Prentice Hall, 1960.

McMahon, Gerard, *Performance Appraisal Skills: Best Practice for Managers*, Oak Tree Press, 1999.

Mooney, Paul, *Developing the High Performance Organisation*, Oak Tree Press, 1996.

Patmore, Bob, *Bob Patmore's Perfect Vision*, Granta Editions, 1991.

Pegg, M., *The Art of Encouragement*, Enhance Ltd., 1995.

Robbins, Anthony, *Unlimited Power*, Simon and Schuster, 1988.

Royce, William S., "How to be a Business Coach", *Journal of Management Consulting*, Vol. 4, No. 2, 1988.

Salisbury, Frank S., *Developing Managers as Coaches*, McGraw-Hill, 1996.

Whitmore, John, *Coaching for Performance*, Nicholas Brealey, 1992.